P9-DSV-319

THE MEROE EXPEDITION

K. A. GRZYMSKI and ALI OSMAN M. SALIH
Directors

MEROE REPORTS

I

by K. A. Grzymski

SSEA PUBLICATIONS XVII

Benben Publications, Mississauga, 2003

Cover Design and Image Layout: Iwona Grzymska

Copyright © 2003 by Krzysztof Grzymski

All rights reserved. No part of this publication may be reproduced, stored in a retrieval system or transmitted in any form or by any means, electronic, mechanical, photocopy, recording or otherwise, without the prior written permission of the copyright owner.

Printed and bound in Canada

dedicated to

Peter L. Shinnie

National Library of Canada Cataloguing in Publication

Grzymski, Krzysztof A. (Krzysztof Adam), 1951-
    The Meroe expedition : Meroe reports I / K.A. Grzymski and Ali Osman M. Salih, directors ; K.A. Grzymski, author.

(SSEA publications ; v. 17)
Includes bibliographical references.
ISBN 0-920168-18-3

    1. Meroe (Extinct city) 2. Excavations (Archaeology)--Sudan. 3. Sudan--Antiquities. I. Salih, Ali Osman Mohmed II. Society for the Study of Egyptian Antiquities. III. Title. IV. Series.

DT159.9.M47G79 2003   939'.78   C2003-905313-X

1. TABLE OF CONTENTS

2. LIST OF FIGURES

All the drawings were made by the author, except for figure 3 (J. Anderson), figures 4a, 4b, 5, 6, 42, 43 (C. Rocheleau), and figures 8, 9, 10 (A. Błaszczyk). Map of Meroe was compiled by I. Grzymska from maps prepared by P. L. Shinnie and R. J. Bradley and by the Meroe Joint Expedition with additions by K. Grzymski.

3. LIST OF PLATES

4. ACKNOWLEDGEMENTS

The fieldwork reported upon in the present publication was carried out under the license issued by the Sudan National Corporation for Antiquities and Museums. We would like to thank particularly Mr. Hassan Hussein Idris, Director General of the Sudan National Corporation for Antiquities and Museums and his colleagues Dr. Salah el Din Mohammed Ahmed and Mr. Salah Omar el Sadiq of the Excavations Section. Mr. Siddig M. Gasmelseed and Mr. Mustafa of the Museum Section were especially helpful in facilitating the access to the Meroe collection in the Sudan National Museum. Additional help and assistance was provided by many other antiquities officers, curators and technicians in the NCAM.

We acknowledge the support of the then Vice-Chancellor of the University of Khartoum Dr. El-Zubeir Bashir Taha and the former Dean of the Faculty of Arts Dr. Majzoub Salim El-Bur. We appreciate the willingness of their successors to continue supporting our project. In the Department of Archaeology we were greatly assisted by Dr. Intisar Soghayroun el-Zein. The project was financially supported by grants received from the ROM Foundation and from the Royal Ontario Museum Department of Museum Volunteers as well as by funds provided by Tilley Endurables and other donors. In the Sudan financial and logistical support was provided by the University of Khartoum. The administrative and visa assistance provided by the Embassy of the Sudan in Ottawa and by the Canadian Embassy Office in Khartoum was greatly appreciated. In the field special thanks go to Mr. Moawia Osman, chief guard of Meroe townsite and Mr. Abderrahim, guard of the expedition's dig-house. Advice and hospitality provided by Canadian geologists working in the Sudan was very helpful. Dr. Hans Onasch and Prof. Steffen Wenig kindly placed at our disposal the updated map of the site prepared by the Meroe Joint Expedition. Dr. Francis Geus and Mr. Bernard-Noël Chagny are to be thanked for giving us permission to use their kite photographs. We are grateful to Caroline Rocheleau and Loretta M. James for their editorial work, to Taber M. James (TMJames Multimedia Services Inc.) for the slide scans and to Iwona Grzymska for preparing the plates and figures. Last but not least we would like to express our gratitude to Professor Peter L. Shinnie for his constant support of our joint undertaking. It gives us special pleasure as his former students to dedicate this publication to him.

Ali Osman M. Salih
Krzysztof Grzymski

5. INTRODUCTION

Recent years saw a dramatic revival of interest in Meroitic archaeology. New excavations have been started at important sites such as Kawa, Jebel Barkal, Musawwarat es Sofra, Naga and others while the research, conservation and reconstruction work at the royal pyramids of Meroe continues. The remains of the city of Meroe have also attracted scholarly attention, but the vast scope of the work required as well as the lack of well documented information from Garstang's excavations presented serious challenges to excavators. In this regard, the Khartoum–Toronto mission was very fortunate in having at its disposal the new publication of John Garstang's excavations prepared by Lászlo Török (1997a; see also Edwards 1999a and Wenig 1999b). This publication also contains references to the post-Garstang investigations at Meroe, personal comments and observations of the author, as well as the presentation of various hypotheses and speculations regarding the archaeology and architecture of Meroe. In the process of exploring the site we were sometimes able to address the issues and to answer the questions posed by Török and other scholars concerning its historical development.

The site of Meroe has been previously excavated by several expeditions starting with the 1909-1914 University of Liverpool mission led by John Garstang.[1] The results of the first campaign were published in 1911 by Garstang, Sayce and Griffith. This publication was followed by a series of interim reports

and annual exhibition catalogues (Garstang 1911; 1912a; 1912b; 1913; 1914; 1914-1916; Garstang and George 1913; Garstang and Phythian-Adams 1914; Sayce and Garstang 1910). In 1997 Török published the above mentioned final report of Garstang's excavations based on the published material and unpublished records held at the University of Liverpool School of Archaeology and Oriental Studies.

A new era of field research at Meroe began with the excavations directed by Peter L. Shinnie first under the auspices of the University of Ghana (1965), then sponsored by the University of Khartoum (1966-1970), and finally as a joint mission of the University of Khartoum and the University of Calgary (1971-1977, 1983-1984). The University of Khartoum was initially represented by Ahmed M.A. Hakem and later by Khidir A. Ahmed. At the time of this writing the final report of the 1965-1972 seasons was published (Shinnie and Bradley 1980) while the second one, devoted to the 1973-1984 campaigns, was in press (Shinnie and Anderson, in press). Preliminary reports of the Khartoum–Calgary joint expedition and other related studies were published by Shinnie and other authors (Shinnie 1974; 1984; 1987; Shinnie and Kense 1982; Ahmed 1999; Bradley 1982; 1984a; 1984b; Robertson 1992; Tylecote 1982). In 1992 the site was investigated by a joint mission of the University of Khartoum, the Humboldt University of Berlin, and the Roemer-Pelizaeus-Museum of Hildesheim co-directed by Steffen Wenig and Khidir A. Ahmed. Several articles reporting the results of the Khartoum–Berlin–

---

[1]For Budge's activities in 1898-1899 see Török 1997a:1 n.5.

Hildesheim Meroe Joint Excavations, which were carried out from 6 to 25 February 1992, were published by Wenig and others (Wenig 1994; 1996; Eigner 1996; 2000; Wolf 1996).

In 1999 the joint Sudanese–Canadian mission to Meroe was revived under the co-directorship of Shinnie's former students, Ali Osman M. Salih of the University of Khartoum and Krzysztof Grzymski of the Royal Ontario Museum. The Royal Ontario Museum has, in the past, financially supported Garstang's and Shinnie's excavations and acquired a small but representative collection of objects from Meroe. In recent years Shinnie has donated his field notes and other records to the Toronto museum. The Khartoum–Toronto expedition began field operations in October 1999 with fieldwork limited to a surface investigation of the site. It was carried out by archaeologists and conservators from the Sudan National Corporation for Antiquities and Museums, the University of Khartoum and the Royal Ontario Museum, namely Grzymski, Dziadowiec and Mustafa. The main purpose of this preliminary research was to assess the present condition of the site and to identify problems and priorities to be addressed by the Khartoum–Toronto mission. In contrast to earlier investigators who concentrated exclusively on research and excavations, our expedition is also concerned with the question of site preservation and protection. These concerns, shared by others, have led to the conservation work currently being carried out at the so-called Royal Baths by conservators from the German Archaeological Institute and the Sudan National Corporation for Antiquities and Museums. It is of utmost importance to realize that in recent years the site of Meroe has become a popular tourist destination. Therefore, it was felt that our research project could not only be limited to excavation but had also to incorporate activities directed at accommodating the increasing flow of Sudanese and foreign visitors.

The present report describes the results of the 2000-2001 season which comprised museum research in Khartoum and Toronto as well as fieldwork at Meroe. The field operations were conducted on three separate occasions: 29 September to 7 October 2000, 2 November to 2 December 2000, and 20 March to 6 April 2001. The construction of a new wall around the dig-house, building of the sanitary facilities and removal of wind-blown sand were carried out during the month of October by the local staff.

Throughout the entire season Krzysztof Grzymski acted as the field director. During the first visit, he was accompanied by Anna Błaszczyk (artist) and Ali Mirghani (NCAM inspector). In the second period of operations Grzymski was assisted by Julie Anderson, Azhari Mustafa, Howeida Mohammed, Caroline Rocheleau (archaeologists) and Mahmoud Soliman (NCAM inspector). Mr. Azhari also supervised, on behalf of Dr. Ali Osman and the Department of Archaeology, University of Khartoum, the renovation and conversion of one of the storerooms into a site museum. In the spring of 2001, Grzymski was accompanied by inspector Ali Mirghani and Awad Suleiman, a builder from the Conservation Section of NCAM.

The site of Meroe suffered in the past from excavations leaving the ruins exposed to wind and rain erosion. Thus, there was no need to rush to excavate it as there is probably no greater danger to the preservation of an ancient site than hasty excavations. With this in mind much time was spent walking over the entire site and recording surface material. This produced a number of pleasant surprises: errors in the published plans of various buildings were identified and numerous graffiti and inscriptions overlooked by previous investigators were noticed. A list of conservation and protection actions needed was prepared. It had been decided, for example, to cut down some trees growing on the walls and to remove at least some of the spoil heaps left by previous excavators. This not only made the site appear more attractive to the visitors but helped re-direct the flow of water away from endangered structures as well as keeping goats from climbing and destroying some of the walls. At the same time new information about the archaeology and architecture of the site was revealed. In the so-called Royal City, that is the area confined within the Enclosure Wall, only surface studies were conducted as most of our activities concentrated in the central part of the site. Excavation and site clearance were carried out at Mound M 712 and at the Amun Temple M 260. The latter is usually the first structure seen by tourists and its appearance bears importance to the Sudanese authorities.

As is commonly known, Garstang numbered various components of the site by using a one to three digit number preceded by the letter M with the exception of the site of Hamadab and some graves where four digit numbers were used. Garstang also published a map of the site (Garstang 1914-1916:Pl. I), which remained in general use until Shinnie's excavations. Shinnie's site map introduced a grid reference system which was used for designating new excavations areas (Shinnie and Bradley 1980:Fig. 3). Additionally, several previously unknown temples along the newly identified processional way were separately numbered in Garstang-like fashion, but prefaced by the letters KC (for Khartoum–Calgary) instead of an M. Another temple discovered by the Sudanese–German expedition was incorporated into the same system but prefaced by the letters MJE (Meroe Joint Excavations), while the three excavation units explored by this team were designated NTA (New Temple Area) 1 and 2 and NW (North West Mound) 1. At the same time, an updated version of Shinnie's map was prepared replacing Shinnie's alpha-numeric grid co-ordinates with a more user-friendly numbers-only system. Additionally, several cement benchmarks were placed at various points across the site. No absolute levels are given for these benchmarks, but with the help of Shinnie's unpublished plans in our possession it was possible to calculate these levels. Part of the MJE map was published in Wolf's article (Wolf 1996:Abb. 1).[2] The need for establishing absolute levels is apparent when one considers that various statements concerning the architectural history of such large building as the Amun Temple were made solely on the basis of the relative position of strata within a trench (Shinnie and Bradley 1980:91-95; Hakem 1988:167) or by means of impressionistic visual observations (Török 1997a:124 and n. 399). This, of course, is also true

---

[2]Only the relative levels are given there with the benchmark 640E/670N set at 10 m (Wolf 1996:30). According to our calculations this benchmark is placed 357.59 m a.s.l.

with regards to other structures and excavation areas.

Our own numbering system follows the KC/MJE grid. Since our work so far has been limited to areas previously identified and numbered by Garstang, that is M 260 and M 712, there was no need to use new designations. Nevertheless, within these existing excavation areas individual contexts (or loci) had to be numbered. These locus numbers were assigned to all the archaeological contexts such as fills, layers, cuts, architectural features, etc. This created a problem with regards to the context numbers used in the Amun Temple where only the rooms were individually numbered. Instead of second-guessing Garstang and trying to retro-fit individual wall and room numbers within his "M" system, all new contexts were simply preceded by the letters AT (Amun Temple), with the exception of rooms M 266a, M 270a, M 273a, and M 274a. These four rooms are shown unnumbered on Garstang's plan. We decided to back-number them with reference to the neighbouring rooms and the addition of the letter "a." Our AT context numbers were assigned to various archaeological and architectural features as the work progressed and therefore are not tied to any specific room or space. Ultimately, the numbering system is merely a matter of archaeological convenience and not a set-in-stone requirement.

6. AMUN TEMPLE M 260

This second largest temple in the Kushite Kingdom and the largest one in the city of Meroe has never been adequately studied. The plans published by Garstang (1911:Pl. III; 1912:Pl. VIII; see also Török 1997: Fig.24) are incomplete and incorrect in many details, yet remain in general use. Hakem modified Garstang's plan by adding a gate in the south wall of forecourt M 271 (Hakem 1988:Fig.20) and Hinkel published more detailed measurements of the Amun Temple, including a new plan of M 270 (Hinkel 1996:Abb. 52) and kiosks M 279 and M 280 (Hinkel 1989:Abb.7 and Abb.12). It seems that the main reason the complete plan was never published is that the temple had not been fully excavated. It is clear from Garstang's reports as well as from his photographs that the temple was excavated from inside out with the debris dumped over and next to the presumed exterior walls. Even within the excavated areas the walls were never fully traced and some elements of the plan are mere conjectures. Still, some of the architectural elements absent from Garstang's plans are so obtrusive on the ground that it is hard to explain why they were never commented upon. This lack of a correct plan and the presence of some unusual features in the architecture of the Amun Temple led many scholars to propose hypotheses which upon closer examination cannot be accepted. Perhaps the reason for some of the oversights and mis-interpretations lies in the fact that while the temple was visited by many scholars, few among them undertook actual research on the site. It is apparent from various publications of Hinkel, Török, Tomandl and Hofmann that some elements of the Amun Temple complex were studied by them during their visits to the site in the last two decades. However, the only recent extensive field investigations have been conducted by Hakem and Shinnie. Hakem, in the course of preparing his doctoral dissertation, visited the site on several occasions between 1966 and 1969 to conduct a surface study of M 260 (Hakem 1988:151). In 1967 Shinnie carried out limited excavations in the southwest corner of the forecourt M 271 and in the doorway leading to the hypostyle hall M 270 (Shinnie and Bradley 1980:91-95). He returned to M 260 during his last field campaign at Meroe, digging several trenches in various parts of the Amun Temple (Shinnie 1987). Due to unfortunate circumstances the original plans and notes of Ahmed and Reed, who acted as the trench supervisors, were not available for inclusion in the forthcoming publication (Shinnie and Anderson, in press). Some of Shinnie's personal records and photographs were recently recovered and passed on to the author with the kind permission to use them in the present report in any way felt necessary. Because of the importance of the work undertaken by Shinnie at M 260 on the one hand and the possibility of various interpretations of Shinnie's observation on the other hand, the author decided to present Shinnie's notes *in toto*. They are attached below as Appendix 6.1. The reader, however, must always keep in mind that these are rough field notes not meant for publication.

The last field season of the Khartoum–Calgary team threw new light on some aspects of the construction history of M 260, but also left many questions unanswered. It was quite evident to us that the first step required was the clearance of the temple in order to study its architectural elements and to draw a detailed plan (plate Ib; figure 2). During the 1999 visit the entire area was cleared of rubbish and other detritus scattered over M 260 (plate II). Grass and bushes were removed and two trees growing on the walls in the north east part of the temple complex were cut down. One of these trees grew over the presumed north pylon. Initial photographic recording of the graffiti, inscriptions, and decorated blocks was also begun. The study and recording of the exposed wall surfaces continued in September 2000 concurrently with the first excavation work, namely the removal of Garstang's spoil heap (AT 5) which was deposited in front of the north pylon AT 4. Additionally, in the following months the internal faces of all the walls surrounding forecourt M 271 were exposed with the view to mapping the interior outline of this area (figure 3). Special attention was paid to the study of the so-called "kinks" in the northeast and southeast corners of M 271. These were partly excavated and drawn. In other areas of M 260 no excavations were conducted and no new trenches were laid out. However, the tracing of wall outlines required removal of sand. The resulting "trenches" were subsequently backfilled with the same sand, although in some instances additional protective measures were also undertaken.

RAMS

It was the four rams placed between kiosk M 280 and the Amun Temple that prompted Garstang to excavate in this area. The rams have been described by Hakem (1988:152-154) and Hofmann and Tomandl (1986:69) and comparisons have been made to the Naga and el Hassa rams which have similar curly fleece. In 1984 Shinnie did some trenching in this area and a brief description of the sondage appears in his field notes (see below appendix 6.1, p. 30). Although Garstang had found only four rams, Lepsius's site plan of Meroe (Lepsius 1849:Pl.132) clearly shows that three pairs of rams once stood in this location. It is unlikely that Garstang would have missed such large sculptures and therefore we can conclude that two rams disappeared some time in the second part of the 19th century. The rams were numbered by us in the following way: AT 50a - northeastern ram; AT 50b - northwestern ram; AT 50c - southeastern ram; and AT 50d - southwestern ram.[3] Rams b, c, and d measured 150 cm x 64 cm each, while ram a was slightly larger at 158 cm x 64 cm. Rams a and b are 5.19 m apart at the south end but only 4 m apart at the north end. Rams c and d are approximately 2 m apart. As Shinnie has already observed, their original position is uncertain (appendix 6.1, p. 30). Presently, northwest ram b is located 13.5 m and the southwest ram d 15.8 m from the centre of the main gate.

SPOIL HEAP AT 5

Ever since Garstang's days at Meroe, two mounds of rubbish fronted the entrance to the Amun Temple. These spoil heaps not only obstructed the view of the front of the temple, they also made difficult the study of the eastern faces of the pylons

---

[3]It must be noted that Hinkel (1996:399) designated the rams "M 257" assigning them one of the numbers not used by Garstang.

(plate Ia). Moreover, the existence of these mounds affected the flow of the rain water, directing it onto the northeastern ram AT 50a and over kiosk M 280. While the kiosk is presently covered by a layer of soil, water seepage may negatively affect the stone blocks despite this protection. The existence of the spoil heaps in the area between the four rams standing east of the temple and the pylons was also preventing the search for possible emplacements for the third pair of rams recorded by Lepsius and Cailliaud (plate IIIa). It is even conceivable that more than three pairs of rams were placed between kiosk M 280 and the entrance to M 260. The removal of the spoil heaps was therefore required as much by the aesthetic as by scholarly considerations. Garstang's north dump was removed to the present-day surface level from an area of approximately 10 x 15 m between the east face of north pylon AT 4 and the northwestern ram AT 50b. The southern limit was formed by the existing passage way leading to the main entrance of the Amun Temple while in the north the rubbish was removed to a point parallel to the north temple wall (plate IIIb).

Excavation of the dump was carried out by a small group of workmen under close supervision of an archaeologist. During the first two weeks all the debris were sieved, but except for an occasional potsherd few artifacts were recovered and subsequently only every third wheel-barrow load was sieved. Only one identifiable object was found, a small circular grinder approximately 4.5 cm in diameter. Other finds included a tiny piece of copper, which might have been a bead but now is simply a lump of metal, and a 13.9 cm long chunk of polished hard brown stone, which conceivably might have been a fragment of a sculpture but is more likely a naturally polished large river pebble. Occasionally, lumps of iron slag were also found in the spoil heap.

This astonishing absence of any finds, apart from the few pottery fragments, may suggest that Garstang's reputation as a careless excavator was somewhat exaggerated and that he did indeed successfully recover all the artefacts to be found in the forecourt M 271. However, it is more likely that the relative sterility of the dump simply reflects the origin of the deposit, namely an open courtyard devoid of objects.

Concurrent with searching for archaeological material, bricks and large brick fragments as well as fragmentary stone blocks were set aside. The redbricks found in the dump were basically of three sizes: 28 x 18 x 14 cm, 32 x 18 x 9 cm and 26 x 24 x 9 cm. These, like the stone fragments, were put aside with a view to re-use them in the restoration work (plate VIb). The remaining sand and soil was transported to the desert by means of a lorry and a donkey cart (locally known as *karro)*. Apart from the architectural fragments, predominantly fired bricks, sandstone fragments and one sandstone column drum 61.5 cm in diameter and 17–22 cm thick were recovered.

The thickness of the spoil dump removed varied from 1 m to 2 m. Upon completion of the work the eastern face of the north pylon was revealed (plate VIa). The outside lining of redbricks was not found on the surface level. It was, however, possible to trace the outlines in a few places where a shallow trench revealed foundation fragments (figure 4cd). No evidence for the emplacement of a third ram was found, but neither was it expected as no trench was excavated between the stone gate AT 2 and the two northern rams.

THE MAIN GATE

The entrance to the temple courtyard M 271 was formed by a monumental masonry gate built of sandstone blocks with moulded corners (figure 3). The two "jambs," as Hakem called them, were numbered AT 1 (south) and AT 2 (north). The floor level inside the gate rises slightly from the present surface level outside the temple. The difference is even more pronounced in the interior of the temple where the present surface level in M 271 effectively forms a depression. The overall impression is that of a double ramp with a slight rise on the outside and a more visible one inside the temple. The present surface level inside the main gate varies between 357.46 m and 357.95 m while the original surface of the flagstones in the second gate between M 271 and M 273 is 356.73 m. We have not yet studied this supposed ramp in the main gate of the temple and therefore we do not know whether it was made of smooth flagstones like those found in the second gate (Shinnie and Bradley 1980:Pl. XXXV). The present surface is formed mainly of small stone chips mixed with sand and soil. Because the base of the stone "jambs" in the main gate is quite high, it is unlikely that any flagstones will be found below the present floor surface. If they were ever placed in the doorway, which is very likely, it must have been done over the present-day floor of sharp, pointy stone chips and small rocks. The width of the passage varies due to the presence of one or perhaps two recesses on each side of the gate, presumably designed for

sheltering the wooden doors when the gate was open. Thus, the width of the passageway on the east side is 3.44 m, inside the recess 3.95 m, while on the west 3.50 m. The presence of one niche on each side of the doorway for placing door wings is clear. Further west, there appears to be another, smaller pair of recesses in the inside walls of the gate. It is difficult to decide whether these were real niches or bays caused by wind erosion of the masonry used in construction. Such weathering is clearly visible in the four corners of the gate all of which presently appear rounded, although originally had right angles (plate IVa).

The two stone "jambs" were studied in some detail by Hakem (1988:155-158), who was the first to observe that their foundations were laid out higher than the floor level of the courtyard M 271 and the adjoining walls. According to our measurements the floor level of the paved sections of M 271 was 356.72 m., while the base of the stone blocks in the west face of AT 1 was 357.62 m. The bottom of the west face of AT 2 was 357.69 m and of the east face was 358.15 m.

The east face of the north side of the gate (AT 2) was not fully exposed. Presently two courses of stone blocks are clearly visible and the top edge of another course is showing above the ground. The lower of the two exposed courses comprises three stone blocks measuring in length 58 cm, 88 cm and 77 cm respectively from south to north. There is a 12 cm gap between the south and middle blocks and a 12 cm deep and 39 cm long recess cut in the northernmost stone. The height of the course is 46 cm and the width of the corner block is 40 cm. Hakem (1988:156) had noticed a few lines cut in the surface and suggested a standing male figure. While his interpretation may be correct, it is important to realize that what is visible is a long, vertical, slightly sloping line cut in the middle block and two parallel vertical lines and a small triangle on the right (north) block. These are presumably traces of a front and back legs and the end piece of a tail or a streamer.

The south face of the north "jamb" AT 2 is made up of four courses of yellow sandstone blocks with seven to nine blocks in each course. The levels of the surface of the top course are 358.71 m in the southeast corner and 359.06 m in the southwest corner. At the west end of the entrance, embedded in the floor in front of the wall is a piece of dark ferricrete sandstone. It is presently impossible to decide whether it has fallen off the gate post, was part of the supposed flagstone floor, or rests in its original position, perhaps as part of the door blocking. No traces of colossal figures mentioned by Hakem (1988:156-158) are presently recognizable.

The interior, or west face of AT 2 has four courses of stones each three blocks wide. Once again a ledge or recess is cut in the northernmost stones to the depth of 15 cm and the length of 46 cm. The total width of the west face is 227 cm and the height up to 170 cm, with individual courses measuring respectively (from top to bottom): 39 cm, 40 cm, 43 cm, and 48 cm. A large figure is incised on the wall with a full, rounded buttock visible in the upper part (figure 4a; plate Va). The back leg is straight, while the forward (south) leg extends diagonally. A line cut at the ankles 26 cm above the base of the foot may depict anklets or the bottom of a long dress. The 112 cm high figure facing

the entrance stands on top of a 6 cm thick line cut 6 cm above the bottom of the lowest stone. At the back a long tail or tassel hangs down to the same level as the supposed anklets, or hem of the dress. Another tassel or streamer hangs farther back (north). It is narrow in its top end, being 2.5 cm wide at the break point, but it widens to 7 cm at the bottom. Fragments of plaster are still preserved.

The south side of the main gate (AT 1), as seen on the west side, rests on at least two layers of redbricks; the upper row arranged as headers, the lower one placed as stretchers. Above this brick foundation are four courses of sandstone blocks, all of them cracked and eroded. The lowest course on the west face is made of two stones only. The north (left) block is 96 cm long and the other is 120 cm long. The south end of this block has a 10 cm deep ledge. This recess, also present in all the overlying blocks, is set 39 cm away from the edge of the stone. The course is 47 cm high and its total length is 216 cm. The second course is made up of three blocks measuring respectively from left to right: 59 cm, 88 cm and 79 cm. The middle block is badly eroded and the south one has the same ledge and recess as the block below. This course, too, is 47 cm high and its total length is 218 cm. The third course is made of three blocks as well but they are all eroded and crumbling. The respective lengths are: 65 cm, 95 cm, and 53 cm with a ledge cut in the last block. The height of the course is 43 cm. The fourth and last course has only fragments of two blocks preserved, the left one being 41 cm long, and the right one measuring 102 cm. The course is preserved to the height of 22 cm. Traces of relief decoration are recognizable on the surface of the three lowest courses (see also Hakem

1988:158). The scene shows a striding figure facing north towards the entrance (figure 4b; plate Vb). The bas-relief is quite clear. The back foot also has traces of plaster attached. The toes of the front foot are missing as the block is broken off at the corner. The distance from the preserved part of the high point of the foot to the back of the ankle is 28 cm. The preserved part of the back foot is 56 cm but originally must have been about 2 cm longer. There seems to be a barely recognizable outline of a diagonally placed sandal strap. A tail or tassel hangs behind the back leg down to the level of the ankle. The preserved part of the back leg as measured from the base of the foot is 93 cm high. The bottom of the front foot is missing and the preserved part of the leg from the mid-foot up is 85 cm. Along the edge on the northwest corner of AT 1 a long vertical line is visible, presumably part of a staff or a spear.

The layout of the north face of AT 1 mirrors the south face of AT 2. The surface level of the top-most course reads 359.25 m in the northeast corner and 358.64 in the northwest corner. On the bottom of the easternmost block of the north face there is a relief of two petals of what seems to be the lotus flower (figure 6b; plate IVb). There is a single straight line extending diagonally to the right (west) of the flowers, probably part of a leg of a person striding towards the west, that is towards the interior of the temple. At the end of this sloping line there are two horizontal incisions, perhaps the fragment of an anklet or the hem of a long dress. Since the higher one of these two lines extends over the blossoms it is possible that the scene showed an individual striding forward over the flowery floor, an arrangement reminiscent of various scenes in the Lion

Temple at Musawwarat es-Sofra (Hintze 1971:Taf.34c). Alternatively, the upper horizontal line represented the bottom of a long dress, the lower line was part of a band or an anklet and the lotus flowers were placed between rather than below the feet of the striding person. The east face of AT 1 is almost entirely covered by Garstang's dump AT 6 and only the outlines of two blocks can be recognized at the moment. A single decorated block with a gently curving line (perhaps top of the head?) incised on its surface lies in the spoil heap about 3 m east of the east face of AT 1.

Hakem (1988:158) suggested that since the proportion of one's foot to the body height is approximately 1/6 to 1/7, the height of the figures in reliefs was about 4 m, and the total height of the gate could have been 5 m.

THE PYLONS

It has been argued by Hakem (1988:154-155) that in the case of the Meroe Amun Temple the term "portal" rather than pylon, which is defined as "a construction of two battered towers which extends a little beyond the width of the court behind it and for which the pylon is a facade," was more applicable. In contrast to the pylon, the portal is a flat wall, without towers, recesses for flagstaffs or inside stairs. It is too early to decide definitely which term is more appropriate, but the existence of the stairways (see below p.11), suggests that the traditional term "pylon" might in fact be applicable to M 260. In any case, the term pylon is used in this report in a general way as a monumental entrance to the temple.

The exploration of the two pylons AT 3 (south) and AT 4 (north) was at first limited to locating and tracing the wall and/or foundation outlines of the interior of the temple. This was achieved in both north and south pylons. They were constructed of redbricks laid in alternating rows of headers and stretchers. The exterior, east face of north pylon AT 4 was further investigated after the removal of the spoil heap. Traces of a brick foundation were found in one section and it was possible to outline the exterior wall of the pylon for a distance of some 6.5 m (plate VIa; figure 4c-d). The exposed length of the actual brick foundation was 3.5 m and in the best preserved part was six courses high. The bricks were abutting a 25 to 30 cm wide row of sandstone chips separating the redbrick lining of the pylon from sandstone blocks of the main gate. At a distance of 3.5 m. north from this row of stone chips there was a niche-like recess in the wall. It was approximately 100 cm wide and 20 cm deep. It remains unclear whether it represented a niche for a flagpost or was simply a collapsed or robbed out fragment of the front wall. While no trench was cut across the thickness of the pylons it is evident from the exposed faces that behind the redbrick lining was a fill composed of mudbricks and rubble. The width of the north pylon was 5.2 m. The length of north pylon AT 4 (including masonry in the gate) measured inside court M 271 was 9 m from the gate to the northeast corner of the courtyard. The distance from the entrance to the inside corner formed by the south pylon AT 3 and wall AT 21 was only 8.30 m. This difference reflects the slight asymmetry of the entire courtyard M 271.

STAIRWELLS AT 20 AND AT 21

Since the main purpose of our work was to trace the wall outlines in order to prepare a proper plan of the courtyard, the sand was cleared only in those parts where the walls were not recognizable on the surface. There were also some instances where a mass of rubble visible on the surface required cleaning in order to define the wall limits. This was particularly true with regards to the abutments visible in the east end of the south and north walls of M 271. The south abutment (called a "kink" by Shinnie, see below, p. 29) has been shown on all the previous plans of the temple. The northern one seems to have been overlooked even though it is quite obtrusive; in fact, it is the highest preserved part of the Amun Temple at 359.61 m a.s.l. The clearance of the walls in both corners revealed that the wall abutments, or "jogs" or "kinks," were in fact long stairwells leading towards the pylons. Since it was not our goal to conduct substantial excavations we stopped our work once the purpose of the structures was made clear and the plan of M 271 corrected.

The south "kink" (AT 21), located in the southeast corner of courtyard M 271, had apparently been explored by Shinnie in 1984 (appendix 6.1, pp. 29-30). The exact dimension of Shinnie's "Trench G" is unclear, but it seems to have covered the westernmost part of the abutment. The structure is clearly a staircase extending for a distance of 14.4 m along the south wall of M 271 from a point where stone wall AT 10 ends and brick wall AT 34 starts. We cleared an area of about 6.5 m long extending from the entrance AT 36 on the west side to the highest preserved step on the east (figure 5b). The entrance, with a stone threshold, was located at the exact place where the stone wall AT 10 comes to the end and the redbrick section AT 34 of the south wall begins (plate VIIb). The width of the stone blocks is equal to the width of two bricks. These bricks abut to and bond with the stone wall. The first two westernmost bricks of wall AT 34 extend along the same line as wall AT 10. Afterwards the wall AT 34 recedes 20 cm southward, the equivalent of one brick. The bonding and the layout of the stone and brick walls AT 10 and AT 34 leave no doubt that they were conceived as an entity and built at the same time. At one point the original entrance to the stairwell was blocked and plastered (figure 5c). The bricks in the blocking measured 29 x 17 x 8 cm. Since there is a break in the north wall (AT 32) of the "kink" it is possible that it was used as an entrance in the later period. There is a slight possibility, however, that this break might have been cut during Shinnie's exploration. His notes refer to "three red brick steps" and "a small room full of occupation debris and a doorway, blocked with red brick, with stone threshold to the west. A large pot had been dug into the bottom step (...)." This seems to be the description of the west part of the stairwell AT 21 The entrance is slightly skewed and not at all at a right angle to the south wall. There is an empty space with sand floor between the entrance and the first step located approximately 3 m to the east of the entrance. The sand floor level is 356.86 m a.s.l., which is slightly higher than the floor in the north "kink" AT 20. Presently only six steps are preserved. The staircase is 128 cm wide filling the corridor-like space between two parallel redbrick walls AT 34 and AT 32. Both the stairs and the walls are made of redbricks measuring 34 x 17 x 10 cm. The four lower steps are a brick-and-a-half deep, that is 52 cm, the fifth step was made of two length of bricks, and of the sixth and last only one

brick depth is preserved. The height of each step varies from 10 cm to 21 cm, with an average of 14 cm. Assuming that each step was 52 cm deep and 14 cm high and considering that the distance between the first step and the junction of the staircase with the pylon is 11 m, the height of the pylon at this point would be approximately 3 m. Whether the stairs ended there or continued within the core of the pylon is not known at the moment. The north wall of the staircase is one brick thick, that is 34 cm. However at the distance of some 6.40 m from the entrance to the stairwell this wall juts out almost 50 cm. Presumably this added thickness was needed to support the weight of the mass of bricks in the stairs.

Shinnie's comments imply that the lowest part was filled with domestic debris including a large pot embedded in the first step. Although no detailed description of this find is available we seem to have found a remnant of this secondary occupation, apparently undisturbed by the 1984 sondage. An accumulation of potsherds, bone fragments, ash and charcoal mixed with sandstone and redbrick fragments was found overlying the third and part of the second steps (plate VIIIa). Among the most interesting sherds was an almost complete, albeit broken, vessel P.9 (figure 30; plate XIIIc). This is Shinnie's form 135, a so-called "candlestick" (Shinnie and Bradley 1980:112, fig. 42; also see below ch. 9, p. 69). Sufficient amount of charcoal was collected to allow C-14 analysis which suggested a *c.* AD 250 date (see table 6-2).

The north abutment, or "kink", AT 20 (figure 5a) was similarly constructed, although the original entrance was slightly narrower (plate VIIIb). It has also been blocked (figure 5d), but there is no evidence for a secondary, side entrance. Although a stone threshold is similar to the one in the south staircase, the blocking is made of sand, soil and redbrick fragments, rather than solid bricks (plate IXa). A flat sandstone block placed on the top strengthens the whole structure. The distance between the entrance and the first step was only 1.06 m and, except for a narrow stretch, the original floor of redbricks was found *in situ*. The level of the floor surface was 356.72 m, which is practically identical with the level of the flagstone pavement in the entrance to M 270 which was 356.73 m. There can be little doubt that this was the level of the main floor of courtyard M 271 and probably of the entire temple. Except for the floor and the first step made of two sandstone blocks, the other steps were not as well preserved as those in the south "kink" AT 21. Fragments of white plaster adhering to the stones were noticed suggesting that the steps of the staircase were plastered. The staircase was a little narrower at 1.2 m while the south wall at 60 cm was almost double the width of its equivalent in AT 21. This south wall thickens by another 60 cm at a distance of some 6 m from the entrance to the north stairwell. An interesting construction detail characterizing this wall was frequent use of large square bricks with curved, finger-impressed lines (plate IXb). Presumably these impressions facilitated bonding. Notwithstanding the use of this special material, the overall impression is that AT 20 was not made as solidly as its southern counterpart. We stopped our exploration after unearthing four steps. There is a good possibility that more steps will be found in this corner which comprises a mass of rubble and mudbricks reaching a height of 359.61 m.

This highest point, which is almost 3 m above the floor level, is located some 3.2 m west of the north pylon AT 4. If we were to use the same measurements as in the south stairway (52 cm for the depth and 14 cm for the height of each step) to calculate the height of the pylon at its junction with the stairs it would amount to 3.8 m.

Although the details and dimensions vary slightly the overall layout of the two abutments within M 271 is identical. Since the bricks of the north wall also bond with the north jamb of the (eventually blocked) entrance there can be no doubt that both staircases form an integral part of the courtyard design. The purpose of erecting such unusually long stairwells within the courtyard is unknown. Perhaps it had something to do with the inferior way in which the pylons were constructed, not allowing for the placement of stairs within the core of the pylons. Alternatively, such stairs were placed within the pylon but only in its upper part, which was reached by the outside stairs. The first solution implies the low height of the frontal structure which could then indeed be considered a portal. The second suggests the existence of a true pylon of substantial height, possibly towering over the stone gate.

NORTH, WEST AND SOUTH WALLS OF M 271

The course of the north wall is clearly visible on the surface and therefore no trenching was required to ascertain its layout, except for an occasional removal of sand and debris piled against the south face of the wall. The north wall comprises three different sections (figure 2):

(1) the redbrick wall AT 46 running for some 14.5 m from the north pylon AT 4 to the west end of the abutment AT 20;

(2) wall AT 11 constructed of redbricks, stone blocks and stone column drums extending for a distance of over 30 m between AT 46 and the north gate;

(3) wall AT 29 which runs for some 12 m between the north gate and the wall (or pylon) AT 26 and which was built mainly of redbricks.

It seems that the redbricks and stone blocks formed only the external casing of the walls whose interior was filled with mudbricks. Further investigations are required to confirm this observation. The exact construction and outline of wall AT 46 also remains to be determined since it is largely hidden behind the stairwell. The best known part of the north wall is the one made of re-used column drums and rectangular stone blocks. Traces of the plaster suggest the spaces formed by the adjoining rounded drums were filled in and the wall surface appeared flat. Shinnie's Trench A cut through the wall and thus revealed the construction details (plate XI). According to Shinnie (appendix 6.1, p. 26), the arrangement was as follows: "The two uppermost courses of this wall consist of re-used sandstone column blocks (...). These sandstone column fragments are resting upon seven, or possibly eight, courses of red brick. (...) Below these brick courses there are about 60 cms of ferricrete sandstone. This is probably the foundation of the wall but these ferricrete slabs rest on two courses of massive sandstone blocks."

In the north gate our research was limited to the visual inspection of the stone faces of the gate. No reliefs were noticed either on the east (AT 31) or the west (AT 30) face. However, a beautifully carved lintel relief of a sun disk surmounted by two uraei was lying in the rubble near the gate (plate XIIb). Judging from the dimension of the gate, which is 2.20 m thick, the width of the north wall was approximately 2 m.

The last section of the north wall was built of redbricks upon which rested sandstone blocks and column drums. Since there are other courses of redbricks on top of the stone layer there can be no doubt that the column drums were deliberately used, or rather re-used, in the construction and were not deposited by Garstang. Careful clearance of the northwest corner of the forecourt M 271 exposed six courses of redbricks in the west wall AT 26, that is the wall between the courtyard and the hypostyle hall M 270. North wall AT 29 was abutting but not bonding with wall AT 26. Moreover, the original white plastering of wall (pylon ?) AT 26 was still adhering to its surface at the place where the north wall was abutting (plate Xa). A similar situation was recorded in the southwest corner where the south wall AT 28 was abbuting but not bonding with wall (pylon?) AT 27. This find is of immense importance because it confirms that the walls presently separating M 271 and M 270 represent the original facade of the Amun Temple. Due to the substantial thickness of these walls, it is likely that they were built as pylons. At some point, a courtyard was added in front of this supposed Second Pylon, the walls abutting what was until then the front facade of the temple. The present state of preservation of walls AT 26 and AT 27, and of the stone facings of the gate (AT 12 on the north and AT 13 on the south) is poor. The upper courses of redbrick were broken and ill-defined. In the process of clearing the north section of the west wall we have found a broken amphora embedded in the floor at a distance of 1.43 m from the north end of the stone facing of the gate (plate Xb). This large amphora was filled with clean, grey sand and immediately to the south of the vessel a small amount of charcoal was found. The radiocarbon dating of this sample suggests a date of about AD 340 (95% probability, see table 6-1).

The doorway between M 271 and M 270 and the southwest corner of M 271 were explored by Shinnie in 1967. This sondage was subsequently published by Shinnie and Bradley (1980:91-96) and also mentioned by Hakem (1988:167). The sondage had been back filled and covered by the wind blown sand. Since neither Shinnie nor Hakem gave absolute elevation of the flagstone pavement, a small 50 x 50 cm square was cleared within the doorway and the levels were taken. The level reading of the surface of two stones was identical, 356.73 m a.s.l.

It has already been mentioned that the joint of west wall AT 27 and south wall AT 28 was cleared and carefully studied revealing the abutment rather than bonding of the two walls. The four brick courses preserved in the corner of the west wall still had patches of the original white plaster preserved. The south wall of forecourt M 271, like its northern equivalent, can be divided into three sections. The western one, AT 28, extending for some 31 m between west wall AT 27 and the south gate, is almost completely denuded. Nevertheless, many of the foundation bricks placed in alternating rows of headers and stretchers were in place and it was possible to identify the wall outline. The presence of a gate in the south wall was first

suggested by Hakem and subsequently such a gate appeared both on the Hakem (1988:fig.20) and Hinkel (1996:Abb.52) plans of the temple. In both instances this gate is placed roughly opposite the west end of kiosk M 279. In reality, however, the gate is located farther east. It seems that Hakem mistook the block with Apedemak graffito for the east jamb of the gate, while in fact this block is part of the west jamb of the south gate. This confusion is fully understandable in light of the field conditions because the debris dumped by Garstang beyond the south wall forms a depression in this very area. Furthermore, a stone rubble immediately east of the Apedemak block gives an impression of a disturbed stone wall. In fact, this rubble is formed by blocks fallen off the gate (plate VIIa). The eastern "jamb" can be identified with two stone blocks with reliefs depicting two large feet striding west, that is towards the gate (figure 6a; plate XIIc). Hakem had, in fact, noticed these feet, but did not associate them with the gate. The actual location of the south gate is opposite the east end of M 279. The east section of the south wall, designated AT 10, is made of well-hewn sandstone blocks still standing two courses high above the redbrick foundation. While the sandstone blocks are not used beyond the line marked by the stairwell abutment AT 21, the layer of redbricks continues all the way towards south pylon AT 3 as part of wall AT 34. This is yet another indication that the entire south wall represents a single construction period. The frequently mentioned splaying of the courtyard walls is more the result of an optical illusion created by the staircase jogs than actual reality. There is, however, a slight deviation from the central line extending from the middle of the main gate to the middle point of the

Second Pylon gate, thus not making the court M 271 a perfect rectangle. The west end of the north wall is about 20 cm further south than the east end of this wall and the west end of the south wall is about 40 cm further south than the east end.

COLUMNS

It is clear from Garstang's photographs that the state of preservation of the sandstone columns in the Amun Temple has deteriorated dramatically over the last ninety years, a result of exposure to the elements. The columns are constructed of layers of composite drums made up of four pie-shaped stone segments in each layer. The original colonnade must have had 30 columns, only 16 of which are extant. The average column diameter seems to be 120 cm, but there was a certain lack of regularity as exemplified in the two remaining columns in the northwest corner, one having a diameter of 124 cm and another only 106 cm. Even the existing columns are fracturing and numerous column fragments are lying on the ground. It has been noticed that the layers of the stone segments in the columns are arranged in a geologically correct order. When fluvial sandstone is deposited, it forms beds with recognizable top and bottom layers. All the extant columns in M 271 are placed with the cross beds in the correct position implying that the Meroites were aware of these depositional beds and maintained their proper orientation even after extracting the stone from the quarries.[4]

---

[4]I would like to thank Mr. Richard Evoy, a Canadian geologist working in the Sudan, who made these important comments during his visit to the site in November 2000.

In the northeast corner of the courtyard, Garstang found a long stone ledge decorated with a series of uraei (Garstang, Sayce and Griffith 1911:12 and pl.V.3; Hakem 1988:160-161; fig.18). We have seen no trace of this ledge, but neither were we searching for it. It has yet to be seen whether this feature remains hidden under the accumulated sand or was dispersed throughout the site in the intervening years. Hofmann and Tomandl (1986:45, Abb.49) reported fragments of a frieze with the uraei on the north wall of the city.

FINDS

The paucity of finds in and around M 271 has already been mentioned. Since our excavation work was very limited, the likelihood of finding many artefacts and ecofacts was low. The few discoveries made were concentrated mainly in the stairwells. Inexplicably, a number of sandstone blocks laying on the surface and clearly exposed to the visitors to the site seem to have been overlooked by previous researchers. Only one block, namely a carved lintel lying on the ground near the north gate has been previously reported (Hakem 1988:159-160). It depicts a sundisc with two uraei carved in high relief (plate XIIb). Four other relief fragments were found scattered between kiosk M 279 and the south wall of the courtyard. Although the location of these four blocks nearer to wall AT 10 than to the kiosk (about 3.80 m south and 2 m east of the southeast corner of the kiosk) would suggest that they were used in the decoration of the south wall or south gate, it is presently impossible to determine their original placement. These small and rectangular blocks were incised in low relief. The identifiable decorative elements included the following:

(1) a sun disc with an uraeus wearing certainly the red crown and possibly a double crown, although this part of the decoration is chipped (figure7b; plate XIIa);

(2) an *ankh* sign and on one side of the block also three rows of short vertical strokes as if used for calculation or marking, clearly not part of the original scene (figure 7a; plate XIId);

(3) fragment of a royal or divine costume (plate XIIIa).

The long lines incised on the fourth and last block must have been a part of a larger scene and could not be identified (plate XIIIb).

Other artefacts found during our investigations of M 271 include a lower part of a large amphora deposited in front of wall (or pylon) AT 26 (P.19; figure 30; plate Xb). This seems to be a secondary deposit placed perhaps at the end of the Meroitic or during the post-Meroitic period. The C-14 date of the charcoal associated with the amphora, AD 340±190, makes both possibilities feasible. By far the largest number of artefacts came from cultural deposit AT 35 in the southeast stairway. It contained a "candlestick" (P.9, figure 30; plate XIIIc), five fragments of a basin (*tashit*) (plate XIIId), six sherds of bread moulds (e.g. P.88, figure 27), five amphora bases (e.g. P.148, figure 27) three bowl bases and four unidentifiable bases, 30 bowl rim sherds, four cup sherds (Shinnie's Fc class), one painted eggshell cup sherd, one black ware bowl rim, five outflaring rims and one straight rim (all six presumably from large bottles; e.g. P.147, figure 29), and five sherds from two different beer jars. Additionally, two beads and a stone pounder were found

during the clearance of wall AT 28 and two more beads were found during the clearance of walls AT 26 and AT 27. A corroded iron nail was found in sand layer AT 49 above the northeast stairwell and a small faience piece was discovered near the south gate jamb AT 39.

ROOM M 270

The hypostyle hall M 270 has not been studied by our team, but attention must be drawn to the fact that the layout of this room is presented differently by Garstang and Hinkel. Garstang's plan shows four columns on each side of the passage way, while Hinkel's drawing has two rows of four columns. This discrepancy came to our attention after the end of the field campaign. It is noticable, however, that these two additional rows of columns are not visible on the kite photographs taken on our behalf by Bernard-Noël Chagny (plate Ib), neither do they appear on Garstang's photographs. Instead, on the south side there is a wall separating M 270 from an unnumbered narrow room, which we designated M 270a. It is now ruined, but certainly cannot be mistaken for a row of columns. The whole matter clearly requires investigation in the field during the forthcoming season.

ROOMS M 266/266a/274

The southwestern corner of the Amun Temple was neither excavated nor cleared by our mission, but it attracted our attention due to large number of graffiti incised on the sandstone blocks in the doorways. The function of room M 266 has been a subject of frequent discussions, although not much had been said about its architecture. Garstang identified it tentatively as a throne room and this identification is still accepted by most scholars (Hakem 1988:109-119,

173-174; Kormysheva 1994:206; Ernst 1999). Török (1997a:122), however, suggested that this "dais room" served as a chapel of Amun-Re and Dieter Arnold (1999:60) connected the "dais rooms" in Kawa and Sanam temples to the New Year's festival courts in Egyptian temples. In terms of the architectural layout of M 266, the plans of Garstang, Hakem and Hinkel differ in small, but important details. Garstang's fails to show the existence of a doorway between M 269 and a pronaos, which we numbered here M 266a (plate XIVa). This omission was corrected by Hakem and the door is also indicated on Hinkel's plan. However, neither of them marks it as being blocked. The bricking up of the doorway took place in antiquity, but the exact date cannot be ascertained at present. Another problematic feature is a wall separating M 266 and M 266a. It appears on Garstang and Hakem's plans as a straight line extending northward from the south entrance to M 266a. Hinkel, however, not only marks it with a broken line but also places it further west, that is receding into M 266. Due to wind erosion and rains, this wall is now hardly recognizable on the surface, but Garstang's photos M.258-M.260 show it quite clearly. Thus, there is no reason to doubt its existence and layout as presented in Garstang's plan. One feature, namely a brick platform allegedly abutting this wall requires further study. Our visual examination suggests that, in fact, it might have been a free-standing structure. While not much can be said about its function, one could venture a guess that it served as a support for a statue of Amun (or Amun-Re).

The main feature of room M 266 is a large dais located in the west end of the chamber. Garstang created much confusion by removing a low, flat sandstone block from the dais and installing a small altar, found in M 267, in its place. The original block is still to be found in the room, buried under the sand. Like a similar, but inscribed block found at Gebel Barkal (Ernst 1999), it must have served as a throne base. As for the alleged doorway in the west wall of M 266 behind the dais, Török has shown convincingly that no opening existed there in antiquity. This section of the wall was simply badly ruined by the time of the discovery and used as a "doorway" by Garstang's workmen during the excavations.

One of the better preserved structures in this part of the temple is a stone gate between the long corridor M 274 and the small room, or pronaos, M 266a. Both "jambs" are covered with numerous graffiti (figures 8-10; plate XV). In this jumble of incised lines, one can discern some identifiable elements such as uraei (figure 10a), a human figure with a fancy headdress (figure 10b), and a giraffe(?) with its head lowered (or an okapi? figure 8). On the east face of the west "jamb" AT 16, there is a five-line long inscription with an incised cross to the left (figure 11b; plate XIVb). It is unclear whether the cross was incised at the same time as the inscription, perhaps to mark the end of the text, or was scratched at a different time. Dr. N. B. Millet has kindly submitted the following comments and transliteration of the grafitto:

The inscription is worn and partly illegible; what seems to be visible is a series of nouns followed by numerals. Some of the nouns appear to follow the pattern of "number x of the y".

wos̩ as̩....se 10
yẹlise s 5
.elise 1 be..
.elise 1
6̣..se

It would seem that the text refers to some sort of an offering.

COMMENTARY

The architectural history of the Amun Temple has been discussed in a number of publications, particularly in the site report by Shinnie and Bradley (1980), in Hakem's book on Meroitic architecture (Hakem 1988), in the conference papers by Török (1984) and by Bradley (1982), and in Török's 1997 book on Garstang's excavations. The large courtyard M 271 played a big part in these discussions. Much has been made of the unusual plan of the colonnade, of the uneven and splayed walls and of the traces of an earlier courtyard which Garstang supposedly discovered in the southwest corner of M 271. It has been long recognized that, if only because of its location, the large courtyard represents the latest stage in the development of the temple (Hinkel 1996:398). The opinions varied, however, as to the actual sequence of events. Török (1997a), apart from postulating the existence of an early Amun Temple within the Royal City compound, basically follows Bradley's (1982:169) reconstruction of the history of M 260 ("the late Amun Temple"). The latter is largely predicated on the supposed existence of a river channel which subsequently silted up.[5] It was suggested that the original courtyard ended "where the masonry portion of the extant north wall ends" (Bradley 1982:169). In the next stage, kiosk M 279, and possibly another kiosk located in front of the temple, were erected. Finally, after the presumed Nile channel silted up, the courtyard was extended eastward with walls made of brick and the original pylons and kiosk were destroyed and replaced by new structures built further east (Bradley 1982:169; Török 1997a:25, 36).

The results of our investigations suggest that no such rebuilding took place. It has been already demonstrated that the north and south walls of M 271 were abutting the previously constructed walls, or pylons, AT 26 and 27. This provided the definite proof for the existence of an earlier, smaller temple to which the courtyard was later added. Even more important was the realization that the walls of the courtyard were bonding with the walls of the newly identified staircases in the northeast and southeast corners. These stairs begin precisely where the masonry walls end and the colonnade changes its course. There is, thus, every indication that the entire courtyard, including stairways and pylons was conceived and constructed as an entity. All the extant columns also seem to be of the same type, irrespective of their location. While there is no indication of the gradual extension of M 271 as it is presently known, the matter of an earlier structure that might have existed in the same location remains an open question. The column drums and

---

[5]Until deep and extensive soundings are carried out to check whether such a Nile channel existed, any speculations regarding this, admittedly attractive, hypothesis would be futile. Wolf (1996:41-46) has already pointed out the difficulties in reconciling the stratigraphy and chronology of structures erected along the Processional Way with the existence of the hypothetical Nile branch.

other hewn blocks used in the construction of the north wall appear to have been taken from some other, earlier building. Gastang's first plan of the temple (1911:Pl. III) shows a broken line in the southwest corner of M 271, presumably depicting an earlier wall or stone floor aligning precisely with the south "kink." Since we now have identified the latter as staircase, it seems that the supposed "early wall" was drawn on the plan as an attempt to reconcile what must have looked to the excavator as an oddly-running wall. The Khartoum–Calgary team excavated in the same general area of the court in 1967 but, unfortunately, their trench did not extend to that area marked on Garstang's plan (Shinnie and Bradley 1980:Fig. 26). Shinnie and Bradley cleared a large swath of brick and flagstone floor in the southwest part of M 271 and in the passage to M 270. They claimed to have found an earlier redbrick floor and a brick "stylobate" on which the columns were placed, all at a level about 20 cm to 25 cm below the main floor level. A different interpretation of this supposed earlier redbrick floor could also be proposed. Close inspection of Shinnie and Bradley's plates XXXIV and XXXV shows the lower bricks to be merely the foundation on which the flagstones and columns were set. Although there are no section drawings and no absolute levels given in the publication of this trench, the depth of the level coincides with the thickness of the stone slabs used in the floor. These we noticed to be about 20 cm to 25 cm thick. Moreover, there is no indication of an early redbrick floor in Trench A, excavated in 1983 and cutting across entire courtyard from kiosk M 279 to the north wall of the temple (appendix 6.1 p. 25; plate XIb).

On the basis of presently available data, we would postulate that there was but a single floor level in M 271. A long passageway made of flat, irregular sandstone blocks went through the entire length of the temple from the sanctuary in the west to the main gate in the east, and perhaps beyond. It is possible that in the open space of M 271 this flagstone processional way stood on a slightly higher level than the floor of the courtyard which was probably made of redbricks or simply sand and hardened soil. In a roofless structure such a raised central passageway would be particularly useful during the rainy season, keeping the elevated floor free of puddles.

In terms of absolute chronology, not much can be added to the previously proposed dates for the construction of M 271 some time between 100 BC and AD 100. The two radiocarbon dates obtained from the samples found near the Second Pylon and on the south staircase are associated with secondary deposit. Such secondary domestic deposits had already been found by Garstang, although often interpreted by him as cremation burials. As Shinnie and Bradley have already pointed out (1980:26), the discovery of such domestic refuse in M 262 implies the collapse of standards and a very undignified use of the temple area. In the case of domestic deposit AT 35 both the C-14 date and the ceramic typology suggest that such a decline had already started in the Late Meroitic period.

The construction history of the main body of the temple is poorly known. The similarity in plan of the Amun Temples B 500 in Gebel Barkal and M 260 in Meroe has been noticed by many scholars and parallels were also drawn to the temples in Kawa, Tabo and Sanam. In his 1984 paper, Török argued for the Napatan date (550-430 BC) of M 260 and pointed out that Garstang, too, dated the original Amun Temple in Meroe to 650-400 BC. Ali Hakem (1988:177) dates the construction of M 260 exlusively on the basis of inscriptions found in the temple and therefore places it at the time of Amanikhabale at the earliest, i.e. around 50 BC. He is, however, somewhat inconsistent in his approach by overlooking the inscribed cippus of Nesmin (Garstang, Sayce and Griffith 1911:13) dated to the 26th to 30th dynasty. In his publication of Garstang's excavations, Török renounced his earlier views regarding the dating of the temple M 260 and suggested that the west rooms of M 260 must have been erected while the Eastern Enclosure Wall of the Royal City was under construction, i.e. mid-3rd century BC (Török 1997a:34-35). As a matter of fact, all the scholars associate the construction of the older part of M 260 with the Enclosure Wall (e.g. Hinkel 1996:397-398). This may seem a logical conclusion, considering that the Amun Temple complex abuts the massive Enclosure Wall. However, a careful look at all the published plans reveals that while the temenos wall of the temple complex and podium M 276 are indeed attached to the Enclosure Wall, the temple itself is not. Its back wall is free standing and separated by a distance of some 7 m from the Enclosure Wall and by about 2 m wide passage M 267 from the podium M 276 which is actually attached to the Enclosure Wall. In this respect it is interesting to note that Shinnie's Trench D/E (appendix 6.1, pp. 27-28) cut east-west from M 261 to M 276 failed to show any direct connection between the back of the temple and the podium. Moreover, Shinnie noted that the foundation course of M 276 was placed

on top of the natural soil and "well above the foundation level of the temple implying that it is later in date." While the whole matter requires further study, one has to be extremely cautious in tying the construction history of the Amun Temple to that of the Enclosure Wall. Even if the latter were in fact erected in the 3rd century BC, one has to consider the possibility that it could post-date, rather than precede the core of M 260. Another problem requiring further research is the development of the core part itself. One notices, for instance, that the walls separating M 273 and M 270 are quite substantial. Do they represent the remains of the first facade of what was once a small temple? If this were the case then, theoretically one could envision not two, but three building phases: (1) construction of a small temple extending from M 262 to M 273, (2) addition of M 270, (3) construction of M 271 and M 279. At present this remains in the realm of speculation, but it also shows how little we know about this largest temple built by the Meroites.[6] The functional analysis of many of the rooms in Nubian Amun temples also needs to be undertaken to explain features which, as has been pointed out, "seem to answer specific Kushite cult requirements of local origin which have no parallels in temples in Egypt" (Arnold 1999:60).

Register of contexts in the Amun Temple

AT 1. South stone gateway of M 260
AT 2. North stone gateway of M 260
AT 3. South pylon of M 260
AT 4. North pylon of M 260
AT 5. Garstang's spoil heap in front of the north pylon AT 4

---

[6]Temple B 500 at Gebel Barkal is larger, but its core part was built by the Egyptians.

AT 6. Garstang's spoil heap in front of the south pylon AT 3

AT 7. Surface in the forecourt M 271

AT 8. North wall of kiosk M 279

AT 9. South wall of kiosk M 279

AT 10. South wall of M 271 between AT 34 and AT 39

AT 11. North wall of M 271, between AT 46 and AT 31

AT 12. North gatepost between forecourt M 271 and hypostyle hall M 270

AT 13. South gatepost between M 271 and hypostyle hall M 270

AT 14. North gatepost between M 270 and vestibule M 273

AT 15. South gatepost between M 270 and vestibule M 273

AT 16. West gatepost between M 266a and M 274

AT 17. East gatepost between M 266a and M 274

AT 18. East gatepost (jamb) between M 274 and M 277

AT 19. West gatepost (jamb) between M 274 and M 277

AT 20. North staircase ("kink") in the NE corner of M 271 between AT 4 and AT 25

AT 21. South "kink" wall/tower in the SE corner of M 271 between AT 3 and AT 36

AT 22. Throne dais in M 271, presently to the west of AT 9 of M 279

AT 23. Cancelled

AT 24. Cancelled

AT 25. Second North "kink" between AT 20 and AT 4

AT 26. Wall between M 271 and M 270, north of jamb AT 12

AT 27. Wall between M 271 and M 270, south of AT 13

AT 28. South wall of M 271 between wall AT 27 and gatepost AT 40

AT 29. North wall of M 271 between wall AT 26 and gatepost AT 30

AT 30. West gatepost (jamb) of the North Gate of M 271

AT 31. East gatepost (jamb) of the North Gate of M 271

AT 32. Inner (northern) wall of the south "kink" AT 21

AT 33. Steps between walls AT 32 and AT 10

AT 34. South (brick) wall of M 271 between wall AT 10 and jamb AT 3

AT 35. Cultural deposit found on stairs AT 33

AT 36. Door blocking on the west end of "kink" AT 21

AT 37. Amphora emplacement on the east side of wall AT 26

AT 38. Soil fill inside amphora AT 37

AT 39. East gatepost in South Gate of M 271 in wall AT 10/28

AT 40. West gatepost in South Gate of M 271 in wall AT 10/28

AT 41. Fill (partly possibly Shinnie's backfill) at the bottom of stairs AT 33

AT 42. Stairs in the north "kink" AT 20

AT 43. Stone floor (last step?) between AT 42 and AT 44

AT 44. Redbrick floor between stone AT 43 and AT 47/48

AT 45. South wall of "kink" AT 20/25

AT 46. North (brick) wall of M 271 between AT 11 and AT 4

AT 47. Doorway blocking on the west end of AT 20

AT 48. Threshold and doorway of AT 20

AT 49. Fill over AT 42/43/44

AT 50. Rams in front of the Amun temple (a) northeastern ram, (b) northwestern ram, (c) southeastern ram, (d) southwestern ram.

AT 51. West stone jamb in a gate between M 269 and M266a

AT 52. East stone jamb in the gate between M 269 and 266a

AT 53. Redbrick blocking in the gate between M 269 and M 266a

AT 54. Flagstone floor in gate between M 270 and M 271 cleared 24.03.01 (first found by Shinnie)

AT 55. Foundation layer of AT 4

CALIBRATION OF RADIOCARBON AGE TO CALENDAR YEARS

(Variables: est. C13/C12=-25:lab. mult=1)

Laboratory number: **152866**

Conventional radiocarbon age[1]: **1770±60 BP**

2 Sigma calibrated result: **Cal AD 110 to 410 (Cal BP 1840 to 1540)**
(95% probability)

[1] C13/C12 ratio estimated

Intercept data

Intercept of radiocarbon age
with calibration curve: **Cal AD 250 (Cal BP 1700)**

1 Sigma calibrated result: **Cal AD 220 to 350 (Cal BP 1740 to 1600)**
(68% probability)

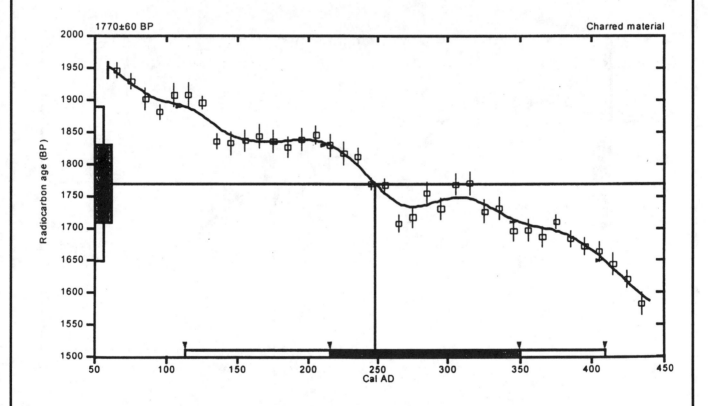

Sample: Meroe 11/2000
Material: charcoal
Location: M 260 AT 35
Laboratory: Beta Analytic Inc., Miami

TABLE 6.1

CALIBRATION OF RADIOCARBON AGE TO CALENDAR YEARS

(Variables: est. C13/C12=-25:lab. mult=1)

Laboratory number: **Beta-152865**

Conventional radiocarbon age[1]: **1700±70 BP**

2 Sigma calibrated result: **Cal AD 150 to 530 (Cal BP 1800 to 1420)**
(95% probability)

[1] C13/C12 ratio estimated

Intercept data

Intercept of radiocarbon age
with calibration curve: **Cal AD 370 (Cal BP 1580)**

1 Sigma calibrated result: **Cal AD 250 to 420 (Cal BP 1700 to 1530)**
(68% probability)

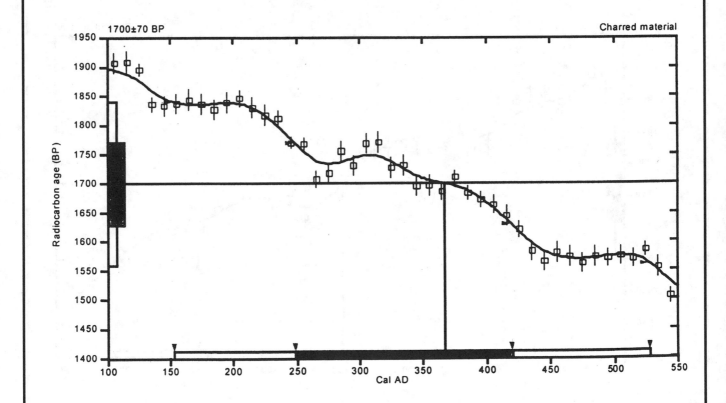

Sample: Meroe 7/2000
Material: charcoal
Location: M 260 AT 26
Laboratory: Beta Analytic Inc., Miami

TABLE 6.2

Appendix 6.1: The 1983-1984 investigations by P. L. Shinnie

The report presented below contains the text of Shinnie's notes describing his work at the Amun Temple. It is important to keep in mind that these were field notes not intended for publication. The text was slightly edited by Grzymski in order to remove typographic errors, repetitions and redundancies.

AMUN TEMPLE

In the final season (1983-1984) it was possible to work in the Amun temple. The original license to excavate had exluded all areas that had been previously worked on (by Garstang) from any new work but in 1983 it was agreed that work might be carried on in the Amun temple (...) and other areas, with the intention of finding out something of the building history of this, the largest Meroitic temple known. Garstang's number system will be used in this report for the various parts of the temple (...).

TRENCH A was laid out 2 m wide at right angles to the north wall of kiosk M 279, with the southeast corner of the trench at the northeast corner of M 279. The cutting extended on a bearing of 30° across the court so as to cut the main north wall of the temple. It is apparent from the photograph (plate XIa) that this trench was eventually extended south, across the interior of M 279. (...)

A detailed interpretation of the deposits in the trench between M.279 and the stylobate suggests the following (...):
Level 1. Post-Garstang fill with a small scoop (...).
Level 1a. Garstang backfill
Level 2. Post use of temple with some slight traces of destruction or collapse - some red brick fragments.
Level 2a. Post-temple floor fill of sterile earth.
Level 3. Thin sand layer level with top of 'apron' to north of M.279 and its pavement. Probably the floor of the temple.
Level 4. Earthy fill with some red brick fragments - either deliberately placed to fill up to planned floor level or, less likely, accumulated through some human activity before the building of M.279 foundation and wall, both of which are dug into it.
Level 5. Sandstone chips on top of brick stylobate and under line of column fragments along its top. The bottom drum of the column visible on the north side of the stylobate has chips up against it and plaster on the column base covers the chips. It looks as though the drums were originally roughly trimmed and only finished in place thus giving rise to a layer of chips which were not cleared from the top of the stylobate after erection of the column. A problem is that in the west face of the section the line of chips very clearly runs south from the level of the top of the brick stylobate and finishes before reaching the foundation of M.279 though on the east face it reaches the foundations. This suggests that [sentence unfinished - K.G.].
Level 6. which looks like a natural accumulation was the ground level when columns were worked on. This level contains some ash streaks and fragments of charcoal suggesting

contemporary occupation. Study of this sequence suggests that the stylobate was built first (level 5) and comes before level 4 and the building of M.279 was added later with the foundation built at the same level as the stylobate foundation just into level 7.
Level 7. Natural soil ("rigeita") into which the foundations of M.279 and the stylobate were slightly dug.

From the stylobate to the main outer wall to north the sequence seems to be:
Level 1. Post-Garstang fill. He did not dig so deeply on the north side of the stylobate but dug straight accross to reach the north outer wall.
Level 2. Destruction level consisting of red brick and sandstone fragments.
Level 3. Not visible but there must have been a floor level (...).
Level 4. Is not there.
Level 5. Sandstone chips separated by a layer of decayed plaster.

The north (outer) wall of M.271 consists of, from top to bottom, a sandstone course, red brick courses, ferricrete sandstone courses and then again sandstone blocks (plate XIb).
The two uppermost courses of this wall consist of re-used sandstone column blocks many with traces of white plaster still adhering to the stone. These sandstone column fragments are resting upon seven, or possibly eight, courses of red brick. One brick in the wall's north face has plaster on an unexposed face showing that it is re-used. Below these brick courses there are about 60 cms of ferricrete sandstone. This is probably the foundation of the wall but these ferricrete slabs rest on two courses of massive sandstone blocks. One of these blocks has plaster on one of the unexposed faces thus showing that it too was re-used. It thus seems that the whole wall is built of re-used pieces giving evidence for the presence of an earlier temple in this area or close by. (...)

TRENCH B (...) was laid out two metres wide at right angles to the south wall of M 271 (...) and its northeast corner was 10.85 m due west of the southwest corner of M 279. The inner face of the main south wall wall of M.271 as seen before excavating was found with a number of blocks lying to the north with fragments of glass bottles the remains, perhaps, of Garstang's stay or perhaps left by later visitors. At the far north end small pieces of sandstone and brick may represent a floor.

(...) The stylobate was made of red brick - only of two courses with the lower one projecting slightly. On the south side of this wall this projection overlies a layer of sandstone chips and rubble. At the east end in the trench a half of the base of one of the original columns of sandstone is still in situ on a rectangular sandstone base. On the north side a hole has been made in the sandstone as though for a door post.
The trench, narrowed to one metre wide was extended to the north to see if there was a stone pavement along the main axis of the temple. It was found there made of sandstone flags with red brick at the north and south ends. It was 7.9 m wide.

Levels in Trench B I (north of main wall)

Level 1. Post-Garstang deposits of wind blown sand. Garstang had found the top of a stylobate column but not its rectangular base. He also went down north and south of the main wall where there is an obvious 'scoop' against the south face.
Level 2. Thin layer representing a level largely removed by Garstang.
Level 3. Destruction level with some brick.
Level 4. Sandstone chips from working of columns and bases as in Trench A.
Level 5. Sandy with some occupation material. This represents the ground level at the time of the working of the column and base. The level was slightly higher to the south where it pre-dates the wall and was the ground level at the time of the wall building.
Level 6. Sterile.

TRENCH B II
(No information regarding its location is available - K.G.).

TRENCH B III was laid out at right angles to B I from the east side to see if suggested pylon could be found. Almost immediately it encountered a small cross wall of irregular pieces of stone running north to south across the trench. It was 70 cms wide at the top with red brick below projecting 10 cms on either side.

TRENCH B IV
Stylobate with channel in it(...).
Level 1. Post-Garstang.
Level 2. Remains of the pre-Garstang deposit.
Level 3. Very slight evidence of destruction level.
Level 4. Sandstone chips.
Level 5. Ground level at time of building.
Level 6. Sterile

TRENCH C. Laid out two metres wide and north to south in M 278 to see what Garstang reached and to see if there is evidence for an earlier building. Garstang shows the south wall of M.278 as being brick. In fact only the upper part is red brick and below it is built of tabular pieces of ferricrete. It is 1.65 [metres] wide. The main outer (south) wall is also of ferricrete pieces with traces of badly damaged mud brick and few fragments of red brick on top and five courses of red brick at the north face. Outside to the south of the main wall is a well made sandstone construction, M.278a, showing a doorway of a separate building with a ferricrete threshold and three threads of steps of red brick leading down to a mud floor. At some time the doorway had filled with sand and then brick threshold was inserted. The foundation of this building below the sandstone has three courses of red brick, then ferricrete slabs, then red brick once more.

TRENCH D/E (M 261, 262, 267). Laid out two metres wide parallel to axis of temple from west of altar stone, across the main west wall of M.260 and across space between it and M.276 (...). The trench goes from M.261 to M.262 and to M.267. There was a stone pavement under 30 cms of recent wind blown sand.

The back (west) wall of M.261 is of red brick, 72 cms wide, with foundation of three courses of red brick laid on edge with one course of stretchers between and a mass of ferricrete fragments thrown into the foundation trench at the south end. (...).

The back (west) wall of the temple is of red brick with deep foundations (1.7 metres). The 'sarcophagus' walls are below this - separated by a layer of 20 cms of sand. The wall is 1.10 [metres] wide. There is an open corridor to the west of the back of the temple wall before the east wall of M.276 is reached as is clearly shown on Garstang's plan. This wall is also of red brick down to the level of a step in the west face of the back wall of the temple. The bottom foundation course is of sandstone blocks on top of a natural deposit of 'rigeita' and it finishes well above the foundation level of the temple wall implying that it is later in date.

TRENCH F. Laid out 2 metres wide parallel to Trench B and with its west side 26.45 metres to the east of the east side of that trench and at right angles to assumed line of south outer temple wall in which three sandstone blocks appear to be in situ

The stylobate wall is of red brick placed on rough sandstone blocks. Parts of the bases of two columns are visible. The west column base has a door socket hole at the north east corner. Further clearing showed that the outer wall had two courses of well dressed sandstone blocks in situ with red brick laid as stretchers below them in the north face. The core of the wall is of undressed pieces of sandstone with some red brick fragments. The south face is of red brick. There is an area of burning just below the top of the stylobate wall to the south.

The main outer wall, as on the north side of the temple, is mainly of red brick. There are five courses of brick on the south with foundations of flat ferricrete pieces, one with plaster as evidence of re-use. The south face has two courses of sandstone slabs, probably re-used, one block certainly is and has a carving of a Meroitic royalty 45 cms long and 27 cms wide. A layer of sandstone chips lies at the level of the bottom of the red brick and certainly represents a ground level on which the masons worked. To the south of this wall is another of ferricrete slabs, probably for a foundation; it is 37 cms deep. The bottom is slightly higher than that of the main wall but the sandstone layer runs over it so it is probably earlier. It is slightly oblique to the main wall. The north face of the main wall is similar. It is constructed of red brick of which six courses remain with ferricrete slabs below and sandstone blocks above.

Stratigraphy in Trench F:
Level 1. Post-Garstang fill.
Level 1a. Garstang back fill at south end only.
Level 2. Post-destruction and pre-Garstang.
Level 3. Destruction level.
Level 3a. Destruction level.
Level 3b. Destruction level (well dug pre-destruction?).
Level 4a. Earthy with brick fragments - represent a construction phase of the temple.
Level 4b. Sandstone chips with earth and perhaps some mud plaster interspersed.

Pre-Temple
Level 5. Sterile windblown sand (...) perhaps the surface at the time of building the temple.
Level 6. Coarse sand with some occupation debris and signs of burning.
Level 7. Sterile sand.
Level 8. 'Rigeita'.

Levels on south side of main outer wall.
Level 1. Garstang's back dirt. He did not dig here but deposited temple fill in this area.
Level 2. Post-destruction and prior to Garstang's deposit of temple fill.
Level 3. Destruction level.
Level 3a. Sterile sandy silt with a line of burning.
Level 3b. Sandy.
Level 4. Sandstone chips - very thick on this south face of the wall.
Levels 5 and 6 as on other face are missing here.
Level 7. Sterile sand.
Level 8. 'Rigeita'.

AREA G. This clearance was made at the south east corner inside M 271 to elucidate the kinks in the wall shown in Garstang's plan. The whole area was covered by his tip but it soon became clear that there was a structure of brick - mostly red but also some mud brick built inside the main outer wall in the corner formed with the east outer wall which is not very clearly seen at this point. There seems to have been a similar structure in the north east corner of the temple courtyard (M.271), though this one, from a rather superficial examination was built entirely of mud brick. This was not excavated nor did Garstang show it in his plan nor describe it and it appears that he did not investigate this corner of the temple.

The south east abutment of this structure is at 7.40m along the inside of the south pylon wall measured from the north face of the south west jamb of the main doorway. Garstang's plan gives it as 7 metres from the same place.

The building first appeared as a very confused mass of red and mud bricks apparently within the main outer wall, though this was far from clear.Since this wall was clear in Trench F rubble was cleared eastwards along it to see where the newly found brick construction joined. The stone upper part of the outer wall of two courses as seen in Trench F runs east for a short distance and then becomes two thin walls of red brick with what is either an earth fill or perhaps a mass of crumbled mud bricks and further east what was certainly a fill of mud brick.This was partly dug out under the first impression that it was part of Garstang's tip thus making it look as though it was a corridor. It was not and must be regarded as a solid wall constructed in this unusual fashion. Certainly a very inferior wall in which to build the main wall of the largest temple in the land. North of this was a massive brick construction running east to the west wall of the pylon. At the west end of this structure three red brick steps led down to a small room full of occupation debris and a doorway, blocked with red brick, with stone threshold to the west. A large pot had been dug into the bottom step and is evidence for domestic occupation. Perhaps the whole construction dates from a period when the temple had ceased to be used for religious purposes and the whole of this bizarre structure was erected for domestic purposes. Such late domestic occupation is clearly shown in temples KC 100 and M 720.

Rams east of the Amun temple

Four rams of the god Amun stood outside the main entrance to temple M 260. They were noted and photographed by Garstang (1911:10,11. Plate VI,1) who describes them as "lying prone in the sand which partly covered them". Since in his photographs they are standing upright, as they still are, he must have put them up. No full description of these rams has ever been given though they have been a well known feature of the site ever since Garstang drew attention to them(...). Each of them had a small figure in front between the upper portion of the front legs - these figures are all very much damaged. The best preserved is on the ram to the north east, the only one which Garstang marks as "in situ", though the meaning of this is not clear if they were all "lying prone". Although the figure cannot be identified with certainty, it resembles Osiris.

Since plinths which might have been for rams had been found in M 271 it was thought that these rams might also have been placed on plinths. Clearance showed rough stone structures beneath them and in a trench dug between the two northern ones there was another stone base made of re-used column fragments. If this was originally a base for a ram perhaps there had originally been three in each row though this does not seem very likely and the arrangement has been somewhat confused since they had been re-erected by Garstang and we cannot be sure of the original arrangement though it is likely that originally there were four arranged symmetrically two by two as Garstang's plan (1911:Plate IV) shows. The base without a ram in the northern group is in line with the eastern ram of the two southern ones. There was no base to the west of the west wall M.280 to line up with the eastern one of the northern group and the original layout must be left unresolved. (...)

ROOM M.270
This is the second court of the temple M.260 shown by Garstang as an open court with eight columns arranged in two rows of four. There was a rectangular construction in the middle which can be seen in a photograph but is not on his plan. Some of it showed through the sand and very little clearing soon revealed it. It consisted of a square flat-bottomed basin (28 cms high) of ferricrete originally plastered with white plaster set on a flat ferricrete base though not quite squarely. It has a small rectangular cut in the south side. The base on which it rests is set into a stone pavement and has a flat-bottomed shallow groove within it (0.25cms deep). The whole assemblage is set in pavement and is surrounded by a rectangular channel completely plastered. A stone pavement runs down the axis of the temple but to the north and south of this east-west axis it is partly of red brick. There are traces of burning on the stone - perhaps squatters' fires or evidence of destruction.

On the north side there is a hole in the pavement with a curved plastered part perhaps for a pole to hold a baldachino. The red brick column bases on the north side are now seen to have been ferricrete with a red brick 'stylobate' between them - this shows on Garstang's photograph but the stone bases do not.

ROYAL CITY

TRENCH H
This trench was laid out along the south side of the Royal City wall at a point where it seems there was a gateway as shown on Garstang's plan. It was laid out ?? m wide and 10 m long. Some stones were visible on the surface which helped in the location. The gateway itself soon became evident and half along the centre line was dug to give a section through it. It became apparent that Garstang had made a shallow scoop to find wall faces and then dug through the gateway to a depth of 50 cms to find the edges of the walls. Below that depth is the undisturbed stratification of the post-gateway fill.

At this point Shinnie's notebook breaks off with a comment added that there should be further description of this trench as it was dug down to the street level through the gateway.

7. MOUND M 712

Mound M 712, which rises almost two metres above the surrounding area, is located near the dig house and the official entrance to the site. The area was apparently investigated by Garstang (1912a:46, Pl.VI; 1914-16:Pl.I) and the depression in the west part of the mound may be the visible result of his sondage. The mound is almost round and measures approximately 40 m in diameter (figure 12; plate XVIa). Its highest point is on the east side, reaching 359.29 m a.s.l. It is located some 20 m to the south of the processional way and about 80 m north of the South Mound. The little information available about Garstang's work on the mound has been conveniently summarized by Török (1997a:177-178). The primary objective for the exploration of M 712 was to establish whether it represented the remains of a temple associated with the processional way or formed the northernmost part of the domestic complex of the South Mound. The chronology of this part of the site also required clarification. An Attic red figure vase fragment dated to 400 BC had supposedly been found here by Garstang together with a painted ceramic lid sherd of local production. Török (1997a:283) demonstrated that the most likely provenance of this red figure vase fragment was in fact M 941, but the matter is far from clear. It was expected that the excavation would help to resolve these uncertainties.

We began our work by excavating a 10 x 10 m square and subsequently expanded by another 3 m on the west and north sides, thus forming a 13 x 13 m square. The original 10 m square extended from 605 m to 615 m north and 700 m to 710 m east on the MJE grid, which is equivalent to line 40.5/T on Shinnie's grid. The 13 x 13 m square comprised the following four units (figure 13):
unit 1 - the original 10 x 10 m square between grid lines 605–615 m N and 700–710 m E;
unit 2 - western extension of unit 1 between grid lines 605–610 m N and 697–700 m E;
unit 3 - northern extension of unit 1 between grid lines 615–618 m N and 700–710 m E
unit 4 - northwestern extension between grid lines 610–618 m N and 697–700 m E.

The entire area was excavated by following the cultural strata. The excavation of a deeply stratified unit containing a jumble of walls, floors, hearths and postholes of what turned out to be a domestic complex is technically very difficult. One can easily understand why Garstang opted for the rapid excavation of monumental buildings. Shinnie, however, was interested in the study of domestic architecture, but with his priority to ascertain the cultural sequence of the town and to establish the pottery chronology he made deep vertical cuts rather than large horizontal exposures. This meant that "(...) the layout of the excavation and lack of time to extend the trenches made it impossible to obtain a complete plan of any single building" (Shinnie and Bradley 1980:25). The advantages of exposing large horizontal units are quite evident when comparing plans of houses excavated in the 8 m wide trench 50-line to those from the 18 m wide trench 79/80-line (Shinnie and Bradley 1980:fig.8 and fig.23, respectively). Only the latter gives us any idea of the dimensions of domestic buildings at Meroe, which were apparently quite substantial. The area excavated so far by the Khartoum–Toronto team is only 13 metres square but some interesting new details regarding the latest phases of site development at Meroe have emerged.

The excavation of mound M 712 is ongoing and the present report is limited to the description of the contents of the excavated square. Future work may revise our present understanding and interpretation of some of these excavated features. The unit comprised numerous walls, rooms, floors and other components suggesting an organic growth of houses (figure 14). The constant process of building, rebuilding, repairing and expanding existing structures, so characteristic of modern Sudanese houses, is also apparent in ancient dwellings as reflected in the archaeological record. This is further complicated by the accumulation of debris and floor levels making the comparison of floor and building levels across the unit a truly onerous task. This helps explain why so few archaeologists undertake the excavation of complex stratified habitation sites in Nubia. In the case of M 712 we can speak of individual levels identifiable within the rooms or in the wall profiles, but these levels cannot always be directly correlated between various rooms or across the site. Since the excavated area was sloping down towards the north, the absolute elevations can be used for guidance only (figure 14). In this interim report, when dealing with

the entire excavated area of M 712, we use the term "level" followed by a Roman numeral to refer to a substantial occupation and/or construction period. In fact, it would be more appropriate to use the term "building phase." However, since the excavation is ongoing it is preferable to reserve the use of the latter term until after the bottom levels have been reached. For the time being the levels are numbered in consecutive order from the top down, with modern surface designated as the first level. Upon completion of the excavations the numbering system will likely be reversed in the final report with the lowest occupation and/or construction phase bearing number 1. This parallel numbering system has been used by Shinnie and Bradley; for example, in the 50-line trench the lowest component (1) is contemporary with the earliest building level VI (Bradley 1984a:199, Table 1).

As for the localised, room-specific occupation levels (layers), they are identified by their respective context numbers. The correlation of these occupation levels across the entire excavated area of M 712 was not always possible; in some parts the stratigraphy was more complex than in others. The terminology and methods used by this author differ somewhat from those of Shinnie and Bradley. Our use and understanding of the term "level" followed by the respective Roman numeral, is reminiscent of Shinnie and Bradley's "component" (in the 79/80-line). One notices, however, that the term "component" has been applied by these authors differently in different contexts. Thus, in the 50-line there were only three major "components" (Bottom, Middle, Top) subdivided into "episodes" comprising "building levels" and "(occupation) levels." In the 79/80-line, however, no use is made of "episodes" and the building levels and occupation levels are grouped into 15 chronological "components." In a subsequent publication, Bradley (1984a:197-207) presented the stratigraphic sequence at Meroe in a different way. The 15 components of the 79/80-line (now called Trench A) became "stratigraphic components" arranged in four groups: Bottom Levels, Middle Levels, Top Levels "Ptolemaic" and Top Levels "Roman." An identical arrangement was introduced in the stratigraphic sequence of the 50-line (now called Trench B). Instead of three components divided into episodes we now have four groups of levels. The old Top Component of the 50-line was subdivided into Top Levels "Ptolemaic" and Top Levels "Roman" and the "episodes" became 11 "stratigraphic components." In the latter case, the equivalencies between the "episodes" and "levels" of the final report and the "stratigraphic components" of Bradley's 1984 paper were not always apparent. Nevertheless, the new format of presenting the stratigraphic sequences facilitated the cross-site comparison of the relative stratigraphy of the cultural material.

The cultural material and stratigraphic sequence identified so far at M 712 suggest that we have here the equivalent of Bradley's Top Levels "Roman" or Shinnie and Bradley's Top Component (50-line) and Components 14 and 15 (79/80-line). The orientation of individual walls in M 712 generally follows the prevalent orientation of domestic structures in the North Mound and the temples in the processional avenue, that is 20°–22° off magnetic north. For the sake of convenience, the direction of walls is given as north-south and east-west, but strictly speaking they are running from northeast to southwest and from southeast to northwest, respectively. The stratigraphic sequence of the excavated units is discussed in chronological order beginning with the earliest presently identified phase, namely Level VI. The majority of the walls unearthed seem to belong to the construction phase of Level IV.

It is interesting to notice that whereas we identified five different construction levels in the top 80–100 cm excavated in M 712, only one episode in the 50-line and one component in the 79/80-line within the top 100 cm were reported by Shinnie and Bradley (1980:Figs. 4, 12). In other words, several of our building levels correspond to the single topmost level in North Mound. This reflects our interest in the minutiae of the latest occupation of Meroe and the possibility of throwing new light on the "end of Meroe" problem. Shinnie and Bradley (1980:69-70) alluded to the existence of redbrick structures postdating their building level I, but they did not elaborate on the subject. These latest structures must have been the equivalent of our Levels II and III. In another publication Bradley mentioned, but did not illustrate, the presence of even later "Post-Meroitic" material (Bradley 1984a:211). Since no actual evidence was presented to support this claim and no Post-Meroitic material was found by the Khartoum–Toronto team at M 712 we can assume that all the latest occupation levels at Meroe date to the Meroitic Period.

Whether one lumps together several late features into a single component, as Shinnie and Bradley have done, or attempts to identify the sub-components, as we have tried to do, is to some degree a matter of interpretation. That is so because when excavating ordinary houses one encounters a series of continuous construction and occupation activities rather than a sequence of discrete, well-defined construction phases. In the context of the late domestic architecture at Meroe the stratification is almost an artificial construct. Nevertheless, in this author's opinion, one can recognize different construction and occupation phases or levels within the M 712 structures. Six levels identified so far could be grouped into four major phases: early redbrick building (Level VI), period of mudbrick constructions (Levels V and IV), followed by late redbrick walls (Level III) and very late squatter occupation (Level II). Modern surface was designated as Level I. The reader must keep in mind that in terms of horizontal division, spaces referred to as "rooms" were so designated on the top plan for the sake of convenience. This top plan, however, depicts almost all the stratigraphic sequences including those during which the supposed "rooms" did not exist (figure 14; plates XVIIIb, XXIa).

LEVEL VI

The earliest recognizable material comes from two different structures (figure 15). In the northwest part of unit 3 a fragment of a very well made redbrick wall was uncovered. Only five bricks of this wall 85 were visible on a level below a later mudbrick wall 94 and the silty fill 77. The bricks were bound with good quality white *jir* mortar. Fill 77 was lying over and next to wall 85. It also sealed the remains of a hearth (*context 80*) containing broken bones, soot-covered sherds, charcoal, small stones, brick

fragments and pieces of iron slag and was covered with yellow sand perhaps used for extinguishing fire. Only part of this hearth was visible; the remainder being embedded in profile line 618 m N. A charcoal sample was radiocarbon-dated to between 50 BC–AD 70 (1 sigma calibration, 68% probability; table 7.3).

If one were to extend eastward the line of temple fronts of KC 104 and MJE 105 it would run some 20 m north of the present north edge of M 712. It is therefore not inconceivable that if there was a temple in this area it would have been located to the north rather than under mound M 712. Only future excavations will clarify whether wall 85, with its strikingly good quality workmanship, formed a back of a temple or some other structure lining the south side of the Processional Way.

In the southwest corner of unit 1 and unit 2, another early feature was noticed. It cannot be directly correlated with the above-described redbrick constructions unearthed in the north end of the excavated area. The present inclusion of stone semicircle 100 and a loose fill of stones, and redbricks fragments, identified as *context 56* (plate XXIb), into Level VI is entirely hypothetical. When seen in the profile line 605 m N its stratigraphic position is by no means clear. It is certainly below Level III, but may be contemporary with Level IV or V.

LEVEL V

Because the north part of the excavated area lies at the end of the slope, the walls were heavily eroded and as a result of the later additions in the centre of the excavated area it is presently unclear whether the hard mud floor 87 in room

"I" is contemporary with a similar hard floor 28 in room "O." Moreover, only further excavation will show whether the supposed rooms "I," "J," "K" and "O" even existed at this stage (figures 14 and 16). This entire area could have been an open courtyard.

Particularly difficult to identify and place in proper stratigraphic order were walls 86 and 88. Wall 86, orientated north-south, was in some sections made of soft sandstone slabs placed vertically, perhaps as a wall lining. These stones are now decayed and can only be recognized as a yellow line. Redbricks were also used placed on their narrow sides as stretchers. This was the west wall of room "I." It abutted another fragmentary redbrick wall 88 which runs east-west forming the north wall of room "I." Associated with these two walls was a hardened mud floor 87 in room "I." Above this floor as well as on the other side of walls 86 and 88 was a silty fill layer 77. Because the area was sloping layer 77 was relatively thin, although a few sherds, some bones and goat (?) hair were found in what was effectively the main occupation layer of unit 3. Further east, several redbricks from an early wall (102) are visible about 50 cm below wall 90 forming the north wall of what became room "E." This wall also belongs to what is effectively the earliest occupation level excavated so far. Because of the environmental erosion, walls 86 and 88 were found only a few centimetres below surface. They were overlain directly by the very late 12-18 cm thick deposit (*context 3*) of dark-grey soil mixed with bones and other refuse. From room, or space, "I" one could enter room "E" which was formed by the mixed mudbrick/redbrick wall 90 on the north, and mudbrick walls 35 (on the east), 69 (west) and 68 and 81 (south). Wall 35 separated room "E" from a small room or perhaps a *zir* area "C" whose northern wall 47 has been only partially exposed up to profile line 710 m E. A *zir* was found under wall 34 on the same level as wall 47. Since wall 34 belongs to the next construction phase (Level IV) it is presently impossible to delineate the supposed *zir*-space "C" within the Level V horizon.

Room "F" was formed by walls 81, 35, 51 and 69. As a result of later rebuilding the east and west walls (57 and 35, respectively) of room "G" are not easily recognizable, unlike walls 51 on the north side and wall 98 on the south. Mudbrick wall 99 of room "K" could have been an extension of wall 98. Whether the break between the two represents an entrance is uncertain. The north-south wall 97 forms the west side of room "K." A later wall 42 is constructed directly above 97 and orientated in exactly the same direction. This phenomenon had been noticed during the excavations of the 50-line, where frequent rebuilding took place "(...) directly on top of earlier structures, the stump of one wall being used as the foundation for a subsequent one, so that there is a great deal of continuity from building level to building level" (Shinnie and Bradley 1980:21).

Other walls belonging to the same construction period were 27, 71, 93 and 82, forming room "O." The north-south wall 71 is attached on its west side to wall 26 for a distance of some 2 m after which it turns slightly eastward. Wall 71 abuts wall 93 which in turn abuts wall 86. Wall 26 is connected to wall 94, the latter placed above and slightly to the south of wall 85 of Level VI. Parallel to wall 27 was a small east-west wall 66 which abutted wall 26. Mudbrick wall 82 is only one brick thick and it runs north-south below later redbrick wall 19/37. Next to wall 82 there was a pottery assemblage comprising, among others, sherds of a saucer/lid, ledge-rimmed bowls and decorated fine wares (e.g. P.79-80, P.137-138, figure 40). In the south-eastern part of unit 1 a mixed layer of organic remains and ash is spread in what became rooms "A," "B" (*context 74*) and "C" (*context 40*). This layer is overlain by later fills 25 and 45 and by wall 46 (figure 20a). Two large storage vessels found in room "A" cut into fill 74 and therefore are later in date. Here too some fine stamped wares were found as well as a snail shell (figure 43; plate XXVf).

LEVEL IV

The general alignment of walls and arrangement of rooms remains the same as in Level V, but in many cases new walls were built on top of the older ones and rooms and/or open spaces were subdivided (figure 17). In the centre of the excavated unit a new wall 37 separating rooms or spaces "O" and "J" was added. Attached on both sides of the southern end of this wall 37 were two platform-like constructions 32 (west) and 52 (east), most probably the remains of stairs or door thresholds. The old wall 69 separating rooms "I" and "E" was replaced by mudbrick wall 92. This new wall did not reach the east-west wall 90 and the opening provided access to room "E". On the south side wall 15 replaced wall 68. Wall 35 probably remained as the eastern wall of room "E" as wall 13 appears to have been built during the Level III construction phase (plate XIXa). Room "F" to the south was now formed by new walls 33 (east), 31 (south) and 36 (west). Puzzling elements are the

stairs in the southeast corner of this room and the postholes cut into wall 31 (plates XIXa, XXb). While the postholes might have been cut during a later period of occupation, the regular arrangement of two of them directly in front of the stairs suggests that they might have been for door posts associated with Level IV construction. The door connected rooms "F" and "G," the latter having the floor on a level higher than room "F," perhaps reflecting the slope of mound M 712. The other walls of room "G" were 33 (east), 58 (south) and 57/44 (west). Two east-west walls 34 and 53 and the north-south wall 48, located in the southeast corner of the excavated area, were also constructed during this phase. Wall 34 seems to have been made of two parallel walls, each one brick thick. The north part, made of redbricks, abuts mudbrick wall 48 forming a room-like space "C." The south part is made of large mudbricks measuring 43 x 21 cm and together with walls 104 and 53 formed a large space which in a later period was subdivided into rooms "A" and "B." In the southwest part of unit 1 rooms "H" and "L" were formed separated by wall 44. Wall 58 was built above wall 98 in room "H" and wall 65 was constructed over the supposed wall 99. At the south end, wall 43 was built more solidly than other walls having a double row of mudbricks, one laid as headers and another as stretchers, forming a brick-and-a-half thick wall (plates XXIb, XXIIa).

The layout of the west side of the unit was changed through the addition of a new east-west orientated wall 96. This new wall abutted the north-south wall 42 which replaced an earlier construction (wall 97). Fragmentary wall 64 in the southwest corner of the excavated area probably belongs to the same construction period (plate XXIIb). The overall appearance of the walls and floor surfaces suggests that this was the main occupation phase of the late period constructions excavated on mound M 712. This impression is further strengthened by the discovery of several large jars placed in the floors of various rooms (plate XIX). Such large jars, embedded into the floor and often with their upper part broken off, were previously found at Meroe by Garstang and Shinnie (Shinnie and Bradley 1980:26). Sometimes they contained charcoal suggesting their use as fireplaces either for cooking or for burning incense. Similarly placed jars were apparently also found at Musawwarat es-Sofra (Edwards 1999d:9).

The majority of objects and potsherds discovered in this level came from fills 38, 39 and 45 in the south and centre of the excavated area. Many were found north of wall 43 in fill 55 immediately below fill 39. Apart from the large number of fine, egg-shell wares, often with stamped decoration (e.g. P.35-P.38, P.40-P.44), sherds of other painted wares (e.g. P.32, P.45-P.48) as well as three sherds of Eastern sigillata (P.85-P. 87) were also found in this level (figures 35-40; plate XXIVe). One very unusual find was a hand-made rim sherd with incised decoration (P.71, figure 26; plate XXVc), perhaps Neolithic.

Several iron arrowheads and a faience tile fragment were found in fill 55 near wall 43 in the southeast area (nos. 52-55; figure 42; plate XXVIe). Additional iron pieces came from fills 38 (nos. 59, 74) and 45 (no. 66). Among the few finds from the north part of the unit the most interesting was a small fragment of a tuyère found in fill 24.

LEVEL III

The most characteristic element of this occupation and construction phase is frequent use of redbricks, possibly taken from some earlier structures. It seems that some of the old walls and rooms were being used, but the accumulation of sand and debris led to the addition of steps and stairs (figure 18). The changes to the north end of room "E" are most clearly recognized. The access from room "I" was blocked through the construction of mudbrick wall 91. Redbrick stairs 12 were added suggesting that by this time sand and refuse had accumulated inside room "E." The north wall 90 and the east wall 13, which was added to wall 33, were also built during this time (plate XIXb). The function of two platform-like structures 20/41 (in room "I") and 84 (in room "O") is unclear; the former might have been a corner pillar and the latter perhaps a door step associated with the fragmentarily preserved late walls 72, 73, and 83. Extending southward from platform 20/41 was a layer of redbricks (wall 19) placed on top of wall 37 and reaching a large stone block A. A similar sandstone block separated rooms "I" and "J" (figure 20b).

There were three other building components belonging to the same construction phase. The well-made redbrick stairs 103 in unit 4 could not be directly associated with any earlier walls, but their placement above the southern extension of wall 26 indicated their late position in the stratigraphic sequence. In the southeast corner of unit 1 a new east-west mudbrick wall 46 (figure 20a; plate XXa) was built abutting the top of the long north-south wall 33, dividing this entire area into two rooms "A" and "B." In the very south end of the excavated unit, between 701 m and 702.5 m E, there was a redbrick wall 63 clearly forming a corner of an unexcavated room south of line 605 m N (plate XXIb).

Associated with these fragmentary wall remains were fills 14 and 16, both composed of a rather hard and gritty soil and sand mix and both probably being the floor remains. Fill 14 was found east of wall 13 and fill 16 was north of wall 15. South of wall 15 and distributed across the entire unit was a layer of gritty dark yellow sand (*context 17*) separating Levels IV and III. All the finds from Level III come either from layer 17 or from fill 14 and include grinders and palettes (nos. 5-11, 45), a bead (no. 67), a possible loom weight (no. 4, figure 41; plate XXVIa) and a small shiny piece of glass or mineral, perhaps galena (no. 50). Some 550 sherds were collected in this level (figures 34-35) as well as a complete saucer/lid (P.6).

LEVEL II

The latest discernible occupation level is represented by a series of flimsy walls made of re-used redbricks and domestic refuse which clustered around the top of, or cut into, earlier walls (figure 19). The poor quality of structures and the nature of finds suggest the squatter occupation by impoverished inhabitants of Meroe. Five loci (*contexts*) in particular can be identified as representing this latest occupation on mound M 712. They were all contained within a layer of dark grey soil (*context 3*) varying in thickness between 12–18 cm and occasionally mixed with sandy layer 2 of Level I. Among the usual domestic remains (nos. 14-21) there was a large millstone with a small palette found next to it (nos. 72-73, plate XXVIb). This suggests that the small flat stones identified as palettes on

which grains or pigments were ground might, in fact, have served as grinders themselves.

Context 4

This deposit was first identified at about 5 to 10 cm below the surface as a rubble of stone and redbricks in the east part of unit 1 between 610.5 to 612 m N and 709 m to 710 m E. The elevation of the top of the rubble is 358.84 m a.s.l. Below the rubble there was a platform-like feature made of mudbricks lined by a row of thick sherds. A mixed deposit that included burnt basketry (*tabak*), charcoal, bones and pottery was approximately 70 cm thick and cut into wall 34. This clearly indicates that the deposit was placed in a pit during the last phase of occupation and certainly after the construction and abandonment of wall 34. The pottery cache contained several ledge-rimmed bowls, a saucer or lid, a potstand and an amphora, a painted bowl, the neck of a beer jar and a fine ware sherd with stamped decoration (figures 31-34; plate XVIIc). The pottery is clearly Meroitic and comparable to that found by Shinnie in his top "episodes." The only other objects found were a thin iron arrowhead, or perhaps a nail, (no. 75; figure 42) and a tiny piece of yellowish foil, perhaps gold, measuring 1 x 0.1 cm (no. 51). There is no indication of any post-Meroitic material. A charcoal sample from this context was radiocarbon dated to AD 140 to 350 (1 sigma calibration, 68% probability; table 7.2). The date is admittedly not very precise but certainly points to the later stages of Meroitic occupation.

Context 11

Located about 3 m south of *context 4* was a rubble, possibly forming a wall (or walls). Two postholes – 21 and 22 – to the southwest and a layer of ash between wall 11 and the east edge of unit 1 are also part of this feature (plate XVIIIa). Wall 11, like the supposed platform in *context 4*, was lined with thick potsherds placed vertically.

Context 9

This locus comprises a row of five redbricks placed on edge in a one-brick thick line. Placed at right angle to these redbricks were four mudbricks placed flat over redbrick wall 63 (plate XVIb). It is possible that the five redbricks were the top-most part of wall 43 re-used by the later occupants of the area. The whole feature is located in the southwest corner of unit 1, separated from *locus 4* by a clean sandy fill 7 running diagonally across the entire unit. A small bowl (P.1, figure 32) and part of the so-called "candlestick" (P.2, figure 34) were found nearby. The "candlestick" was placed upside-down covering a small amount of charcoal. The sample was collected but remains to be dated.

Context 10

A slight discolouration of soil and a little ash in *context 10* indicate fire, perhaps a hearth. An assemblage of tools such as a whetstone, pounders, grinders and grinding stones or palettes (nos. 24-26, 29-36; plate XVIIb) was mixed with complete and broken ceramics (including two saucers or lids P.3, P.4) and some animal bones, giving the impression of the meal leftovers (plate XVIIa). This "kitchen deposit" does not seem related to any of the late structures, simply floating within sand *context 8*. The whole deposit is grouped over a small area of some 30-40 cm, 358.57 m a.s.l., between 700.90-701.20 m E and 611.40-611.70 m N. Perhaps the most interesting aspect of this entire assemblage was the fact that the tools found attest to a well developed sense of aesthetics; the palettes were clearly selected by colour: off-white, red and yellow; the last one also depicting a human face (plate XVIIb top centre). A piece of banded agate might have been a pounder or was simply collected for its beauty. The charcoal collected in this context produced a somewhat unexpectedly early C-14 date of AD 60 to 220 (1 sigma calibration, 68% probability; table 7.1).

Context 54

A redbrick rubble less than one metre in diameter was found about 25 cm below the surface directly above wall 26 from which it was separated by the sand and fill layers 17 and 25. Since some of the bricks were set on their narrow side they might have been part of the wall foundation. The bricks measured 30 x 17 x 7 cm.

LEVEL I

This is the topmost level comprising both the surface and the 5 cm to 8 cm thick layer of yellow sand mixed with grey organic and inorganic detritus such as sherds and brick and slag fragments. It is deepest on the west side of the unit and in the northeast corner. No features were recognizable and all the material from this level must be considered highly contaminated. Four diagnostic sherds were collected in this level (P.74, P.125, P.139, figure 31; P.76, figure 26). One of them, an amphora fragment P.139, was probably an Egyptian import.

DISCUSSION

The late occupation phase strata excavated by the Khartoum–Toronto team were studied in some detail because very little is known about the latest inhabitants of Meroe. In terms of archaeological material we have the Post-Meroitic remains found by Garstang in the cemeteries, but as no contemporary material was reported on from the settlement, very little can be learned about the latest inhabitants of Meroe city from his reports. Török (1997a:39), after studying Garstang's unpublished records, simply stated that the final period in Meroe is almost completely unknown. The physical appearance of the latest mudbrick houses found by Garstang (Török 1997a:Pl.173) is somewhat reminiscent of the M 712 structures. The dating, however, remains uncertain.

The report of the Khartoum–Calgary excavations mentioned "(...) fragmentary traces of a redbrick building level post-dating building Level I" in the 79/80-line trench and "(...) mudbricks, lumps of dried mud, and isolated flecks of charcoal" in Trial Trench 5 (Shinnie and Bradley 1980:69-70). The evidence for the latest occupation at the site was summarized by Bradley (1984a:210-211) as follows: "Sparse surface traces of redbrick structures worn down to a single course were common on the north mound, often differently oriented than the structures in the trenches. The carpet of redbrick rubble over the mound, where the excavated structures were almost exclusively of unfired brick, suggests that an entire component may have been robbed and eroded away. (...) In the newly-excavated temples were found numerous indications of squatter occupation, including grindstones, improvised hearths, and sherds of coarse 'Post-Meroitic' pottery." This description could just as well be used to summarize the material found in the top levels of M 712. It must be stressed, however, that neither at M 712 nor in the Amun Temple

have we noticed any Post-Meroitic pottery. Moreover, such pottery is absent in the published ceramic corpus of the Khartoum–Calgary team. The clearest scenario for "the end of Meroe" was proposed by Roberston (1992:46-49). His strongest argument in favour of the Axumite conquest and destruction of the city is provided by the evidence of violence, fire and destruction recognizable in the small temples cleared by Shinnie during the 1975-76 season (M 282, M 720, M 104). Roberston also suggests that the flimsy redbrick remains were built by the Post-Meroitic settlers who scavenged the building material from the Royal City. While the Axumite presence is corroborated by the discovery of stelae and coins, there is little doubt in the mind of this author that the decline of the city began much earlier. All the material recovered in the top levels of M 712, and indeed from the top levels of Shinnie's and Garstang's excavations, is exclusively late Meroitic. The radiocarbon dates point, in the opinion of this writer, to the gradual decline of Meroe starting as early as 250 AD. The major structures went into disuse, some were probably destroyed by the army of Aezanes or his predecessors (Kirwan 1960:167), but the surviving remains must have been used for sheltering local population, certainly terminal Meroitic and perhaps Post Meroitic, for an extended period of time. The late deposits found by us in the Amun Temple seem to support this interpretation. Some of the vessel forms, particularly the so-called "candlestick" (P.9 figure 30; plate XIIIc; Shinnie and Bradley form 135) are clearly late. Shinnie's "candlestick" was found in the top-most level of trench H50. Three fragments from Musawwarat es-Sofra, ZN 777, ZN 778 and ZN 785 (Edwards

1999d:26 and Pl. IX), are probably slightly earlier. A footed stand from W.106 (Dunham 1963:194 and fig.140a) is dated to the generation 60-70, i.e. 200-300 AD. Another example comes from Garstang's tomb 800 (Török 1997:274 and Pl. 236). The dating of this tomb is uncertain and may very well be of the mid-third century AD. In the end, it is not a single vessel form that determines the dating but the entire assemblage of material including ceramics, small finds, standard-sized Meroitic bricks and, last but not least, the C-14 dates, that points, in my opinion, to the early decline of the city of Meroe. In some way, this development parallels that of Rome where the once prosperous imperial capital gradually contracted in size. In Rome the final blow came with invasion of the Goths and the Vandals, while in Meroe it was delivered by the Axumites.

Register of context numbers in M 712

1. Surface layer of sand, bricks and sherds; level I
2. Top sand layer, 5 cm to 8 cm thick; level I
3. Layer of soil mixed with organic material; level II
4. Mixed bricks & stone cluster within layer 3; level II
5. Orange-red sandy fill; level II
6. Brown fill of mixed sand and organic material below layer 3 in the east part of unit 1; level II
7. Wind-blown sand fill (equivalent of layer 2) abutting and under layer 3; level II
8. Brown fill of mixed sand and organic material below layer 3 in the west part of unit 1; level II
9. Flimsy redbrick wall in the southwest corner of unit 1; level II
10. Domestic assemblage ("kitchen refuse") at c. 701 m E line; level II
11. Flimsy redbrick wall in the southeast corner of unit 1; level II
12. Redbrick stairs between rooms "I" and "E"; level III
13. Redbrick and mudbrick wall running north-south; level III
14. Fill east of wall 13; level III
15. Mudbrick wall running east-west and abutting wall 13; level III
16. Fill north of wall 15, equivalent of fill 14; level III
17. Layer of gritty, dark yellow sand mixed with sandstone particles, running across unit 1, south of wall 15 and under fills 6, 7, and 8; it separates levels III and IV.
18. Large soot/charcoal stain, probably a hearth, abutting wall 11 on its east side, and continuing westwards below the wall; level II?
19. Redbrick wall running north-south; it seems to be the addition of wall 37; level III
20. Fragment of a wall or platform extending 1 m southward from the north profile of unit 1 (= 615 m line); this is part of wall 41; level III or IV
21. North posthole in the southeast part of unit 1; level II
22. South posthole in the southeast part of unit 1; level II
23. Fill in the northwest corner of unit 1, west of walls 19 and 20; level IV
24. Fill below layers 17 and 14 east of wall 13, north and west of cluster 4, south of wall 15; level IV
25. Sand layer overlying floor 28, but under fill 23; level IV
26. Mudbrick wall running north-south in the northwest corner of unit 1; level V
27. Mudbrick wall running east-west in the northwest part of unit 1; level V
28. Mud plaster floor in the northwest part of unit 1; level V

29. Fill in rooms "I", "J" and "F"; level IV

30. Fill south of, abutting and partly above wall 27, possibly equivalent of fill 23; level IV

31. Thin mudbrick/redbrick wall in the middle of unit 1; level IV

32. Redbrick/mudbrick feature over wall 27 and west of wall 31; level IV

33. Mudbrick wall running north-south in the northeast part of unit 1; level IV

34. Wall running east-west from wall 33 up to and below feature 4; level IV

35. Small mudbrick wall in the northeast corner under fill 24; level V

36. Small wall between wall 31 and 15; level IV

37. Redbrick wall running north-east and forming south part of wall 19; level IV

38. Brown, organic fill, above sand layer 25, south of wall 31 in the centre of unit 1, perhaps equivalent of fill 23; level IV

39. Brown fill, above sand layer 25 in the southwest part of unit 1; level IV

40. Ash-rich fill in the southeast part of unit 1 below layer 25; level IV or V

41. Redbrick platform (= wall 20) abutting wall 19; level III or IV

42. Mudbrick wall running north-south near the west limit of unit 1 (line 700 m E), below fill 38; level IV

43. Wall running east-west between walls 42 and 44 in the southwest corner of unit 1; level IV?

44. Wall running north-east parallel to wall 42 in the southwest part of unit 1; level IV

45. Fill in the southeast area, below wall 11, equivalent of fills 38 and 39; level IV

46. East-west wall in the southeast area abutting and over fill 45; level III

47. Mudbrick wall running east-west under fill 24, abutting wall 35; level V

48. North-south mudbrick wall below fill 24 and feature 4, west of the 710 m E line; level IV

49. Floor (*mouna*) north of wall 51; level V

50. Fill in the southwest corner below wall 9 and fill 39; level IV

51. Mudbrick wall running east-west along wall 31 between wall 33 and platform 52; level V

52. Platform or pillar at the south end of wall 37; level IV

53. Mudbrick wall running east-west in the southeast corner of unit 1; level IV

54. Redbrick rubble along the 700 m E line and above wall 26; level II

55. Organic fill north of wall 43 containing numerous bones and sherds; level IV (below fill 39) or late level V

56. Fill with rocks in the southwest corner of unit 1 abutting wall 43; level V or VI

57. North-south wall between walls 51 and 58; level V

58. East-west wall, parallel to wall 51, running from wall 57 to wall 33; level IV

59. Fill layer below 2 and 3 in unit 2, abutting walls 43 and 42; level II or III

60. Animal skeleton in unit 2; level II?

61. Fill in unit 3 abutting walls 13 and 62, equivalent to fill 14; level III

62. North-south wall in unit 3, extension of wall 13; level III

63. Redbrick wall or abutment, below (or base of) wall 9 and above wall 43; level III

64. Wall rubble west of wall 42 and south of 60; level IV?

65. Wall between walls 42 and 44; level IV

66. Flimsy mudbrick wall running east-west, parallel to wall 27; level V

67. Hearth cut into the south face of wall 51; level III or IV

68. East-west mudbrick wall under wall 15; level V

69. North-south mudbrick wall under stairs 12; level V

70. Fill in the northwest part of unit 3; placing uncertain, levels II-IV?

71. North-south wall east of, and parallel to, wall 26; level V

72. Redbrick wall running east-west in unit 3; level III

73. Redbrick wall running east-west in unit 3, northwest of wall 72; level III

74. Fill in the southeast corner of unit 1 below fill 45; level IV or V

75. Subsurface organic layer in unit 4, equivalent to layers 2 and 3; level I

76. Sand fill in the west and southwest part of unit 4, equivalent to sand layer 7; level II

77. Fill in the northeast part of unit 3, below layers 2 and 3; level V

78. Fill layer in central part of unit 4 above wall 26; level III or IV

79. Fill/rubble in the north and northeast part of unit 4; level II/III

80. Part of a hearth deposit along the 618 m N line in unit 3; level VI

81. Fragment of an east-west mudbrick wall under wall 68, possibly part of wall 35; level V

82. Mudbrick north-south wall under wall 19/37, but slightly to the west; level V

83. Thin east-west wall representing an extension of wall 73; level III

84. Wall or platform east of wall 72, south of wall 83 and west of wall 20/41; level III

85. Solid redbrick wall running east-west below wall 73 in the northwest corner of unit 3; level VI

86. Traces of a wall of decayed sandstone slabs running north-east, abutting walls 84 and 41; level V

87. Hard mud floor (*mouna*) abutting walls 86 and 88; level V

88. Flimsy wall running east-west below fill 77 and abutting walls 86 and 89; level V

89. Redbrick platform or wall abutting wall 88 and the 618 m E line; level V

90. Small east-west wall between walls 13 and 91; level III (or IV?)

91. Mudbrick door blocking north of steps/rubble 12 and wall 92 and over wall 69; level III

92. Mudbrick wall abutting steps/rubble 12 and over wall 69; level IV

93. Mudbrick wall oriented east-west in unit 3 abutting wall 71 but under wall 72; level V

94. Mudbrick wall oriented east-west, abutting wall 26 and below wall 73 in units 3 and 4; level V

95. Mudbrick wall oriented east-west next to, but on lower level than wall 64; level V

96. Mudbrick wall oriented east-west, extending from wall 42 to the west face of unit 3, i.e. line 697 E; level IV

97. Mudbrick wall oriented north-south and under wall 42; level V

98. Mudbrick wall running east-west as an earlier phase of wall 58; level V

99. Mudbrick wall or mastaba extending east-west north of wall 65; level V

100. Line of stones in the southwest corner of unit 1 and southeast corner of unit 2; level VI

101. Mudbrick wall or bench along the west face of unit 3; level IV or V

102. Redbrick wall under later wall 90; probably level V

103. Redbrick stairs in unit 3 above wall 26; level III

104. Mudbrick wall running north-south between walls 46 and 34; level IV

105. Southernmost extension of wall 33 near the south end of unit 1; level II or IV?

CALIBRATION OF RADIOCARBON AGE TO CALENDAR YEARS

(Variables: est. C13/C12=-25:lab. mult=1)

Laboratory number: 152863

Conventional radiocarbon age¹: 1890±60 BP

2 Sigma calibrated result: Cal BC 10 to Cal AD 250 (Cal BP 1960 to 1700)
(95% probability)

¹ C13/C12 ratio estimated

Intercept data

**Intercept of radiocarbon age
with calibration curve:** Cal AD 110 (Cal BP 1840)

1 Sigma calibrated result: Cal AD 60 to 220 (Cal BP 1890 to 1740)
(68% probability)

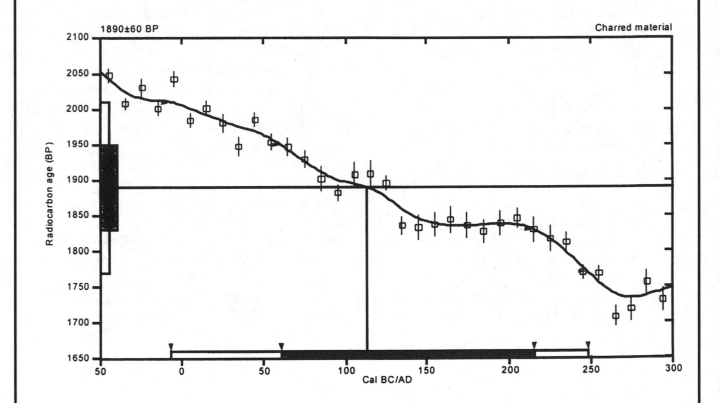

Sample: Meroe 5/2000
Material: charcoal
Location: M 712 [10]
Laboratory: Beta Analytic Inc., Miami

TABLE 7.1

CALIBRATION OF RADIOCARBON AGE TO CALENDAR YEARS

(Variables: est. C13/C12=-25:lab. mult=1)

Laboratory number: **152864**

Conventional radiocarbon age[1]: **1780±70 BP**

2 Sigma calibrated result: **Cal AD 80 to 410 (Cal BP 1870 to 1540)**
(95% probability)

[1] *C13/C12 ratio estimated*

Intercept data

Intercept of radiocarbon age
with calibration curve: **Cal AD 240 (Cal BP 1710)**

1 Sigma calibrated result: **Cal AD 140 to 350 (Cal BP 1810 to 1600)**
(68% probability)

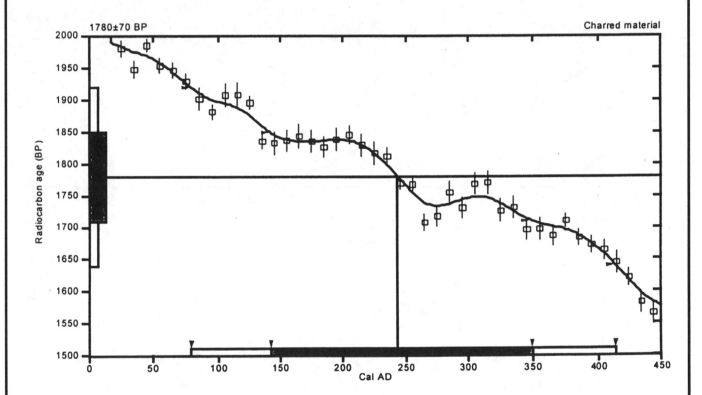

Sample: **Meroe 6/2000**
Material: **charcoal**
Location: **M 712 [4]**
Laboratory: **Beta Analytic Inc., Miami**

TABLE 7.2

CALIBRATION OF RADIOCARBON AGE TO CALENDAR YEARS

(Variables: est. C13/C12=-25: lab. mult=1)

Laboratory number: 152867

Conventional radiocarbon age[1]: 1990±60 BP

2 Sigma calibrated result: Cal BC 160 to Cal AD 130 (Cal BP 2100 to 1820)
(95% probability)

[1] C13/C12 ratio estimated

Intercept data

Intercept of radiocarbon age
with calibration curve: Cal AD 20 (Cal BP 1930)

1 Sigma calibrated result: Cal BC 50 to Cal AD 70 (Cal BP 2000 to 1880)
(68% probability)

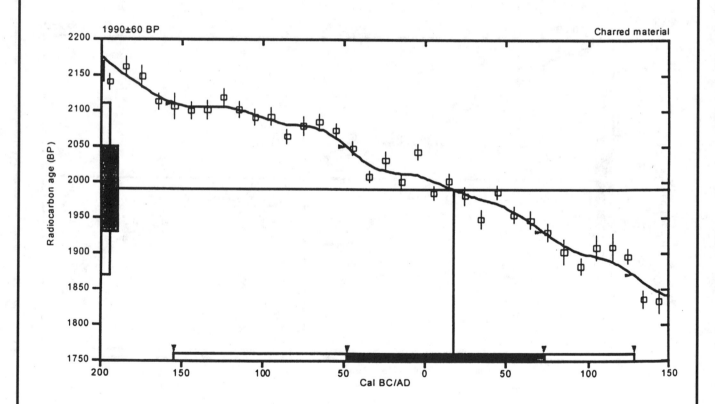

Sample: Meroe 12/2000
Material: charcoal
Location: M712 [80]
Laboratory: Beta Analytic Inc., Miami

TABLE 7.3

Appendix 7.1: Animal remains by C.S. Churcher

Six small bags of bone samples from M 712 were shipped to Toronto. The bone fragments were submitted to Professor C.S. Churcher for identification and the following is his report:

The animals present, in order of numerousness, are cow (*Bos taurus*), goat (*Capra hircus*), ass (*Equus asinus*), probably hartebeest (*Alcelaphus buselaphus*), and a 'pig,' either pig (*Sus scrofa*) or warthog (*Phacochoerus aehtiopicus*). A shell fragment of the Nile oyster (*Etheria elliptica*) is also present.

Cow (*Bos taurus*) is the most numerous in the number of pieces and at least seven individual are present in the samples. Ass (*Equus asinus*) is well represented by pieces, but all are from one individual. Goat (*Capra hircus*) is represented by a juvenile thoracic vertebra; hartebeest by a blackened longbone shaft fragments; and the possible 'pig' fragment by a rib shaft. The Nile oyster is represented by a fragment of a valve.

All the animals are to be expected from a site in the Nile Valley in Holocene times. The many pieces of cow probably reflect the more robust nature of the bones of cattle and that they, therefore, resist degradation more strongly. Most of the bones have suffered degradation from the high temperature of the soil in summer, and a few are blackened, charred or calcined, indicating fire. No persuasive evidence of cut marks or green breaks was observed. Thus, dismemberment may not have been very skilled or may have involved the use of mauls to break longbones and cutting only through fleshy parts. The ass may have been a body of a dead animal disposed of in a midden. Adult and juvenile cattle are present, and possibly one bull on the evidence of a massive vertebral fragment.

This small sample fits well into the fauna listed by Carter and Folley (1980).

Samples contents list

Sample #1: M 712 Pot X

Goat (*Capra*), caput humeri, juv.
Rib shaft, skull fragment (?)
Cow (*Bos*) acetabular rim, scapular fragment, both juvenile
Hartebeest (*Alcelaphus*) longbone fragments
plus
bone scraps, possible bird rib (?) Size of a large chicken

Sample #2: M 712 [70]

All large animals, weathered, possibly from a hearth.
Cow (*Bos*) caput femoris.
Distal epiphysis, right subadult, radius and ulna
Large longbone shaft fragments
Pig (*Sus*)? Rib, anterior

Sample #3: M 712 [39] and [40]

Bull (*Bos*) odontoid and collar of axis
Cow (*Bos*) shaft fragment, calcined, humerus, three (one lower two upper) molar
fragments, two juvenile
rib shaft fragments and distal end anterior rib
neural spine, bone scrap
All cattle, but one bull, one adult cow and one calf with unerupted permanent teeth

Sample #4: M 712 [4]

All ass/donkey (*Equus asinus*)
Distal end left humerus and shaft fragments
Proximal end left radius, shaft fragment
Proximal end left metacarpal III and phalanx I left
Tibial shaft fragemnt
Vertebral scrap; scapula fragment

Sample #5: M 712 [55]

Nile oyster (*Etheria elliptica*) fragment
Goat (*Capra*), thoracic vertebra, juvenile
Cow (*Bos*), fragments from

> right dentary
> Right M3 and Rt. M? newly worn
> left astragalus
> left acetabulus
> right side phalanx II
> right side phalanx I
> left side phalanx I
> right calcaneum, juvenile
> lumbar vertebra, juvenile
> femur, shaft fragment
> scapula, glucoid and blade
> rib fragments
> right side phalanx III
> sacrum
> distal humerus anterior (charred)
> metapodial (?)
> thoracic vertebra - juv. ?*Capra*

Sample #6: M712 [59]

All cow (*Bos*)
left navicular cuboid
right side phalanx II
left femur, juvenile
vertebral spine base
rib fragments.

8. ROYAL CITY

The area contained within the monumental masonry of the Enclosure Wall is commonly referred to as the Royal City. The jumble of bricks, stones, architectural fragments, walls, ramps and streets makes it truly confusing. Garstang's extensive and rapidly executed clearance of this area uncovered a maze of streets and buildings whose detailed architectural history will require many years of study by archaeologists. Our present activities in this part of the site were limited to assessing the state of preservation of various structures within the Royal City. In the process we made a number of observations that supplement the information provided by Garstang and Török. One of the most intriguing parts of the Royal City is its central section with the ruins of buildings, or palaces, M 294 and M 295. The condition of the two buildings has deteriorated somewhat since Garstang's excavations through weathering and the destructive impact of tree roots to the stone slab and loose stone rubble walls. This conservation problem will have to be attended to in the future. Despite the natural erosion, it is still possible to trace the outlines of some of the walls. We noticed with great interest some discrepancies between Garstang's plan (see Török 1997:Fig.2) and the actual course of the walls.

M 294

The outline of the north wall, which is made of stone slabs and rubble, is still visible. The wall is 2.2 m wide and currently stands about 1 m high above the surface. The north part of the west wall is also visible and one can see the partly preserved brick lining running along the edge of the top of the wall. The situation is more confusing in the central and southern part of the west wall, particularly in the section located vis-a-vis the northeast corner of M 295. At first, we mistakenly believed that several stone blocks formed the east lining of the east wall of M 295. In fact, these blocks represented the west facing of the west wall of M 294 with some white plaster still adhering to the blocks. The south wall presumably continues under the dump mounds in its western and central parts, but is visible near the east end. The south section of the east wall is untraceable on the surface. Perhaps it is to be found under the sand and brick mound, presumably a dump heap left by Garstang. The broken line delineating the southeast corner of M 294 on Garstang's plan suggest that its state of preservation was already poor at that time. The east wall, however, is quite well preserved in its northern part which still stands approximately 1 m high. It is made of the usual slabs and rubble partly resting on stone blocks and what looks like column drum fragments. About 12 m south from the northeast corner of M 294 and projecting eastward are the remains of what seems to be part of a monumental gateway, or maybe a tower, built of sandstone blocks. This is not marked on Garstang's plan. The whole structure extends for about 4.3 m along the east wall and projects about 5.8 m on the north side. The south side is only about 3 m long and it remains unclear whether it is the result of the increased thickness of the east wall or simply accumulation of debris. It seems that a small, enclosed chamber was located within the walls of this projecting structure.

Garstang's plan shows a small hall with four columns slightly off the centre of M 294. Only one column is now visible on the surface. Approximately 15 m east to southeast of this column hall are remains of an interior gate with stone jambs 50 cm to 60 cm wide and 24 cm thick and a door 120 cm wide. The entrance is flanked on its south side by two more blocks approximately 70 cm long and 36 cm thick, and placed at a right angle to the jambs and at their far ends thus widening the passage to 142 cm (plate XXIIIa). This stone gate was not marked on the plan.

Numerous stone fragments, including column drums, can be found strewn to the north of M 294; a higher concentration is visible near the northeast corner of the palace. The ground slopes gently in this part of the city, but rises again further north to what looks like a dump heap from the excavations of M 292.

M 295

The east section of the north wall is presently covered by sand and brick detritus and not easily recognizable on the surface. The northwest corner, however, can be identified. It is constructed of sandstone blocks overlain by rubble and slab stones of various sizes, but generally no larger than 20 cm x 30 cm x 5 cm. Numerous sandstone blocks and two column drums are lying loose on the ground in the northeast corner of M 295. One block, measuring 44 cm x 35 cm x 17 cm, has a clearly incised cartouche of Anlamani (plate XXIIIb; figure 11a). In the top part of the block two *t* signs, presumably of the *nsw-*

bity title, can be seen. Within the cartouche signs *Imn-in* are fully preserved and a small depression just above the break-point is clearly the head of a lion, i.e. the *l* sign. There can be little doubt about the identity of the ruler, but nevertheless it is puzzling that the name is preceded by *nsw-bity* instead of the usual *s3-r^c*.[7]

The entire west and south section of M 295 is flat and empty and the southwest corner cannot be recognized on the surface. There is a wall extending eastward from M 95/195 and almost joining the south part of the west wall of M 295. This wall does not appear on Garstang's plan. The main interior structure is quite well preserved with a small stone tank presently lying outside the west wall. Many re-used column drums can be seen in what is either a free-standing wall or, more likely, a podium, on top of which stands the actual building. Török (1997a:162) too considers M 295 to be a "podium-like" structure and compares it to M 294 and the palace of Amanishakheto at Wad ben Naga. There are a substantial number of buildings constructed in this manner in Central Sudan and it certainly warrants further study. It cannot be simply dismissed as a natural accumulation of material from earlier structures re-used in new buildings (Ali Hakem 1988:183). Apart from possible religious significance, at least in the case of temples, and the influence of the Greek

---

[7]There are, of course, examples of Napatan kings using two different titles for the same name, such as Aramatelqo in his spacers from M 294 (see Török 1997a:Fig.119, inscriptions 12 and 16), but to the best of my knowledge this has not been the case with Anlamani.

architectural models, one must also consider environmental factors. Perhaps these temples and palaces were constructed on the platforms to protect them from water entering the interior of the building during the rainy season. One can easily imagine the streets of the Royal City filled with the rain and flood water that could take days or weeks to recede. The question of Meroitic urban planning and its adaptation to the prevailing environmental conditions is a major research problem and cannot be addressed in this report.

9. POTTERY AND SMALL FINDS

The present report is very much a work-in-progress and its main purpose is the prompt presentation of finds rather than an in-depth analysis. The material discussed below comes mainly from M 712, with the addition of the few objects found in the Amun Temple. Pottery was the single largest group of finds. Initially, complete or almost complete vessels were included in the objects catalogue. This proved cumbersome and impractical and eventually all ceramics were catalogued separately, but a few vessels were given object numbers. In the following description, the object number in the pottery section is provided next to the pot number for reference only.

POTTERY

The ceramics sample from the Khartoum–Toronto excavations is relatively small. There were a total of about 3,300 sherds found in M 712, in an area 13 x 13 m wide and 0.3 m to 1 m deep, and less than a hundred sherds in the Amun Temple. This contrasts sharply with the over one million sherds unearthed each year by Shinnie at Meroe (Shinnie and Bradley 1980:151) and even with the 24,200 sherds found in a single season at Musawwarat es-Sofra (Edwards 1998:62). These two publications together with the work of Seiler (1998; 1999) form the core of the Meroitic pottery corpus from domestic sites in Central Sudan. Additionally, we have two assemblages from cemetery sites, namely Gabati (Rose and Smith 1998) and the royal cemeteries of Meroe (Dunham 1957; 1963). Considering the domestic context of our material, the most important comparative collections are those from Meroe and Musawwarat. Unfortunately, because of a different way of presenting the material it is sometimes difficult to make direct comparisons. Shinnie and Bradley opted for the straightforward visual presentation of forms combined with the verbal discussion of fabrics. A more detailed analysis of pottery forms from the Khartoum–Calgary excavations was prepared by J. Robertson and E. Hill for the forthcoming report (Shinnie and Anderson, in press).[8] These authors reduced Shinnie and Bradley's 145 forms to 20 form classes, such as lids, bowls, cups, storage jars, etc., and provided a wealth of statistical data. Edwards, on the other hand, arranged his material primarily according to the fabrics (wares) and then grouped the forms within his wares categories. He made no attempt to reconcile his classification with that of Shinnie and Bradley, perhaps because he considered the latter to be a "perfunctory publication" (Edwards 1999d:38). Moreover, in his opinion the descriptions of Meroe F wares "are not detailed enough (...) and cannot be used to make meaningful comparisons with the Musawwarat material" (Edwards 1999d:27). In spite of this somewhat harsh judgment, the reader of Shinnie and Bradley's report can extract a lot of useful information from the Meroe publication. Interestingly, Edwards' fabric classification, largely based on

---

[8]I would like to express my gratitude to Dr. Robertson for sending me a copy of the manuscript. While it was too late to incorporate the results of his work into the present report it will certainly facilitate the processing of pottery in future seasons.

Seiler's study, seems to confirm Shinnie and Bradley's classification, which distinguished four main wheel-made fabrics and four hand-made fabrics. The comparison of ware descriptions in these two publications clearly shows the following equivalencies: Meroe fabric B = Musawwarat fabric A.2; Meroe fabric C (especially Cc and Cd) = Musawwarat B.1; and Meroe fabrics Fa and Fb = Musawwarat C.1. Meroe fabric Fc ("imitation of *terra sigillata*") is, according to Shinnie and Bradley, Adams' Family M Ware R 35, while Edwards (1999d:27) refers to the Meroe F types as Adams' Wares W 26 and W 35. Török (1997a:285) lists them as Adams' Wares W 26 and R 35. There were few handmade vessels at Musawwarat, all identified as fabric A.7. The descriptions in the two publications are not precise enough to establish the equivalencies and it seems that Musawwarat A.7 = Meroe fabric J and fabric K. The ware identification becomes a little more confusing when one takes into consideration descriptions provided by Seiler who, unlike Edwards, provided direct references to Shinnie and Bradley's work. According to her, Meroe fabric B is equivalent to Musawwarat fabric A3, while Meroe fabric C = Musawwarat fabric A2. Finally, Meroe fabric K = Musawwarat fabric A6. In light of these differences and considering that the publications of Meroe, Musawwarat es-Sofra and Gabati each employ their own classification systems, the creation of a concordance of fabrics and forms from various sites in Central Sudan ought to be a priority for ceramologists.

In order to facilitate comparison between our pottery and the ceramic material from the Khartoum–Calgary excavations the presentation of the Khartoum–Toronto material generally follows a similar pattern. The vessel forms are arranged using the criterion of openness/constriction, i.e. open shapes precede constricted shapes. On the other hand, efforts were made to group the forms into larger categories, as was done by Edwards and Robertson and Hill. It must also be pointed out that in our present recording system we used a number of forms not separated in the Robertson and Hill's classification, e.g. bases, saucers, "diskettes" and *doka*. Since we are still in the process of developing a satisfactory classification scheme, it is possible that we may also introduce *zir*, *qadus* and basin (*tashit*) as separate vessel forms. While every effort will be made to maintain Shinnie's and Robertson's classifications we reserve the right to arrange the pottery classes in a manner that suits best our needs and reflects progress made in the study of Meroitic ceramics.

The processing of pottery at habitation sites in the Nile Valley is always a major problem. The use of *turiya* in excavation leads to the breakage and loss of many sherds, particularly the smaller and finer ones which might skew the statistical value of frequency calculations. The bigger problem, however, is not that of missing a few sherds, but of how to process the thousands or millions found on a given site. During our excavations at Meroe all sherds were collected in plastic bags and rubber buckets labelled according to the findspot (context) numbers. The preliminary sorting took place on site, with diagnostic sherds such as rims, bases, handles, decorated and/or unusual body sherds collected for further study. Ordinary body sherds were counted and discarded on site. The majority of retained sherds and complete vessels were catalogued, drawn and photographed. Following Shinnie, we used the register number prefixed with "P" for cataloguing ceramics from M 712 and Amun Temple. In contrast to Shinnie, however, our pottery registry included not only the complete vessels, but also rims, bases and decorated or unusual body sherds. So far 153 pots and potsherds have been registered, but since many of them were identical in form and fabric only 121 were drawn. All the drawings are presented in this report (figures 21-30).

Shinnie and Bradley have identified seven fabric types subdivided into 28 ware varieties grouped according to surface treatment, colour and decoration (Shinnie and Bradley 1980:151). The supposed eighth fabric, P, seems rather elusive and although the authors suggested a prehistoric date (or prehistoric tradition) for such wares, no specific form and pot examples were given. It is possible that our unusual sherd P.82 (figure 28) might belong to this fabric category. While Shinnie and Bradley considered their classification as purely preliminary, our observations fully confirm the validity of their fabric typology. It must be noted, however, that the nuances of colour and fabric are often in the eye of the beholder. Having personally examined some of the sherds published by Shinnie and Bradley, this author would occasionally classify them in a different way, e.g. Shinnie/Bradley P.120 was identified as fabric Fd, but it seemed more like fabric C. On the other hand P.50 was described as fabric Bb and P.171 as fabric Cc, but in fact the fabric of both vessels is identical. Clearly, at this stage at least, the pottery classification based on form typology is the preferred way of dealing with ceramics from Meroe. In terms of fabric typology we retained Shinnie and Bradley's categories such B, C or F, but found it difficult to distinguish between various sub-groupings, such as Ba, Bb, etc. It must also be pointed out that Shinnie's fabric Fd is not really part of the F class which, properly speaking, comprises only the vessels made mainly or exclusively of kaolin. Finally, when comparing our vessels with those published by Shinnie and Bradley the readers must be alerted to the fact that these authors often use different scales even within the same figure. All the drawings in the present report are in scale 1:3 and when comparing the figures and vessels in the two publications appropriate adjustments must be made. Since Shinnie and Bradley presented their vessel forms only as drawings it was felt that in order to facilitate the use of their publication for making comparisons with pottery discussed in the present report the concordance of the pot forms, pots and fabrics ought to be compiled from their figures and pot descriptions (see Shinnie and Bradley 1980:98-151). The form number is followed by the pot number and fabric type.

1. P.242 Cc; P.349 Cc
2. P.160 Cc
3. P.10 Cc; P.16-18 Cc; P.27-28 Cc; P.43 Cc; P.44 Ba; P.124-126 Bb; P.135 Bb; P.140 Cc; P.145 Bb; P.155-158 Bb; P.161 Bb; P.178 Cc; P.241 Cc; P.246 Ba; P.287 Cc; P.323 Cc; P.350 Bb; P.375-377 Bb
4. P.399 Ba
5. P.300 Ba
6. P.243 Ba
7. P.11 Jc; P.31 Ka; P.132 Ka; P.164 Ja; P.165 Kb; P.180-181 Hc; P.388 Ka
8. P.128 Cc

9. P.95 Cd
10. P.217 Cc; P.225 Ba
11. P.87 Cc
12. P.398 Ba
13. no example
14. no example
15. P.89 Cc
16. P.297 Cc
17. P.405 Ca
18. P.187 Cc; P.340 (no fabric listed)
19. P.101-102 Ba; P.211-212 Ba; P.397 Ba; P.402-403 Ba
20. P.94 Ba
21. P.152-153 Ba; P.224 Ba
22. P.117 Cc; P.223 Cc; P.367 Cc, P.379 Cd
23. P.199 Ja; P.303 Cc
24. P.118 Ka; P.390 Ba
25. P.172 Bb; P.184 Bb; P.189 Hc; P.202 Bb; P.203 Ba; P.222 Bb; P.304 Cc; P.310 Bc; P.368 Bc
26. P.248 Cc; P.250 Ba; P.256 Ba
27. P.25 Ba; P.318 Ba
28. P.50 Ba
29. P.30 Cc; P.81 Bb
30. P.6 Cc; P.9 Cc; P.143 Ce; P.185 Cd; P.245 Cc; P.249 Cc; P.341 Cd
31. P.38 Ce; P.47 Ce; P.51 Cd; P.79 Cd; P.119 Ce; P.179 Ce; P.209 Ce
32. P.34 Cc; P.347 Cd
33. P.24 Ba; P.238 Cc; P.279 Bc
34. P.14 Cd; P.373 Ka
35. P.198 Kd; P.285 Cb
36. P.321 Kc
37. P.53 Cc; P.139 Cd; P.163 Fc; P.174 Cc; P.177 Cc; P.188 Cd; P.192 Cd; P.306 Cc; P.372 Bb
38. P.138 Kc; P.151 Fa; P.358 Cc
39. P.173 Cd; P.346 Cd
40. P.382 Cc
41. P.41-42 Cd; P.46 Cc; P.130-131 Cc; P.159 Cc; P.175 Cd; P.176 Ce; P.194 Cd; P.208 Cd; P.348 Cd
42. P.21 Ce; P.23 Cd; P.37 Cd; P.90-91 Ce; P.134 Cc; P.169 Ce; P.255 Cc; P.305 Cc; P.369 Cd; P.386 Cc

43. P.7 Ce; P.12 Cc; P.35 Cc; P.92 Cc; P.121-122 Cc; P.133 Cc; P.154 Cc; P.226 Cc; P.237 Cc; P.247 Cc; P.356 Cd; P.360-363 Cc; P.365 Cc
44. P.15 Cd; P.52 Cd; P.129 Cc; P.141-142 Cd; P.144 Cd; P.146-147 Cd; P.227 Cc; P.364 Cd
45. P.54-55 Cd; P.62 Cd; P.69 Cd; P.263 Bb; P.293 Cd; P.336 Bc
46. P.380 Cc
47. P.182 Kb
48. P.307 Jc
49. P.338 Bb
50. P.171 Cc
51. P.22 Ce; P.230 Cc
52. P.26 Cd
53. P.107 Cc
54. P.231 Q?
55. P.342 Cd
56. no example
57. P.1 Cd
58. P.345 Kb
59. P.127 Cc
60. P.197 Cc
61. P.2 Ja; P.36 Ba; P.88 Ja; P.137 Cc
62. P.204 Bb; P.205 Bb
63. P.39 Ja; P.301 Cc
64. P.5 Fc; P.210 Ja; P.216 Fc
65. P.3-4 Fc; P.319 Fc
66. P.351 Fa
67. P.86 Fc
68. P.166 Fa
69. P.193 Ja
70. P.195 Ja
71. P.162 Kb; P.186 Jc; P.396 Cb
72. P.113 Cb
73. P.110 Ba
74. P.73 Bb; P.75 Ba; P.215 Bb; P.308 Bb
75. P.228 Ja
76. P.150 Jc
77. P.80 Jc; P.214 Fc; P.244 Cd
78. P.30 Ja; P.191 Jc; P.254 Bb; P.275 Jc; P.292 Jc
79. P.67-68 Ja; P.71-72 Ja; P.74 Ja; P.76 Ja; P.83 Ja; P.100 Cc; P.233 Ja; P.236 Ja;

P.251 Cc; P.252 Ba; P.311 Ca; P.325 Ca; P.401 Ca
80. P.229 Ba; P.270 Ba; P.343 Ba; P.393 Ca
81. P.65 Jc
82. P.196 Cc
83. P.207 Cb
84. P.56 Cd; P.57 Cd; P.66 Cd; P.190 Cd; P.201 Cd; P.206 Cb
85. P.213 Ka; P.391 Ke
86. P.253 Jc; P.296 Jc
87. P.200 Ke
88. P.355 Cc
89. P.395 Fd
90. P.58 Cd; P.99 Cc
91. P.40 Hc
92. P.45 Jc; P.82 Jc; P.264 Jc; P.294 Je
93. P.167 Kd
94. P.20 Hc
95. P.109 Fd
96. P.96 Cb
97. P.103 Hc
98. P.266 Be; P.271 Bb; P.273 Bb; P.277 Bb; P.332 Bb; P.357 Bd; P.384 Bb
99. P.406 Bb
100. P.111 Fd
101. P.112 Bb
102. P.183 Bb
103. P.64 Bb; P.108 Bb; P.291 Bb; P.326 (fabric not listed)
104. P.123 Bb; P.281 Ba
105. P.85 Be; P.232 Be; P.333 Be; P.374 Be
106. P.239 Qa
107. P.49 Qa
108. P.267-269 Be; P.272 Bb; P.283 Bb
109. P.218 Bb; P.359 Bb
110. P.29 Bb
111. P.60 Be; P.284 Be; P.290 Be
112. P.404 Ha
113. P.240 Hc; P.280 Hc; P.330 Hc
114. P.282 Hc; P.329 Hc; P.392 Hc
115. P.61 Ba; P.262 Bb; P.316 Bb; P.334 Bb; P.381 Ba
116. P.309 Be; P.312 Ba; P.327 Cb
117. P.104 Ba

118. P.48 Bb; P.149 Bb; P.258-259 Bb
119. P.383 Bc; P.385 Bc
120. P.77 Bb
121. P.260 Bb
122. P.278 Bb
123. P.84 Cb; P.219 Cb
124. no example
125. P.33 Kc
126. P.220 Cc
127. P.168 Cd
128. P.120 Fd
129. P.97-98 Bb; P.105-106 Bb
130. P.114 Bb
131. P.400 Ha
132. P.59 Ha
133. P.366 Hc
134. P.328 Ba
135. P.8 Bb
136. P.136 Cc; P.353 Ha
137. P.331 Hc; P.335 Hc
138. no example
139. P.298 Fd
140. no example
141. P.148 Kc
142. P.317 Be
143. P.288 Bd
144. P.320 (fabric not listed)
145. P.221 Ka

The approximate relative frequency of various form types can be estimated from the number of vessels listed above under the specific vessel form. In the present report the quantification of vessels is based on calculating the total rim sherd percentages establishing the minimum vessels counts (e.g. 321% of added rim sherds implies a minimum of four vessels). The discussion of the Khartoum–Toronto material follows the order of figures. Unless stated otherwise all the vessels listed were wheel-made. Findspot lists the location (chiefly M 712), followed by the context number. In the pottery and small finds description the following conventions are used:

L = Length, D = Diameter, W = Width, Th = Thickness, H = Height.

I. Saucers or lids

These small vessels were identified by Shinnie and Bradley as saucers (forms 1-3). All but three of these pots were listed as form 3, although the form type shown in the drawing seems a little too deep. In fact most of these "saucers" are like our dish P.4 (figure 21) or Edwards ZN 729 (Edwards 1999d:Pl.VIII).

The function of these small dishes has been a matter of conjecture. In the Shinnie and Bradley pottery catalogue they are initially listed as saucers, but beginning with the 1968-69 season the description refers to "a saucer or pot lid" (eg. P.124). Coincidentally, the fabric identification also changes from C to B, which might suggests that a different individual processed the pottery. The Khartoum–Toronto examples seem to be mainly of the C fabric (= Edwards B.1), i.e. mixed silt and clays. Three examples were listed in the Musawwarat publication (Edwards 1999d:25), one being of the B.1 fabric (ZN 729), while the other two representing local fabric H.1. Edwards considers these vessels to be jar lids pointing out that their diameter is equal to that of the mouth of the so-called beer-jars. Robertson and Hill also call them lids. Since no mud was ever found attached to the base of these vessels, it is likely that the "saucers" were used simply for covering rather than sealing the beer-jars. They might have been in fact of dual use, that is serving both as jar mouth covers and as small open dishes.

During our excavations we found four complete vessels and sherds of several more dishes, all apparently of fabric C. These were as follows:

P.3, (= object no. 48) disk-shaped saucer/lid, complete vessels with worn interior showing brown fabric C, exterior red-slipped, rounded-bottom, D: 9.7 cm, H: 2 cm; M 712[17] (figure 21).

P.4, (= object no. 49) disk-shaped saucer/lid, complete vessel with interior and exterior red slipped, fabric C, flat bottom D: 10 cm, H: 1.5 cm; M 712[11] (figure 21).

P.12, disk-shaped saucer/lid, complete vessel with a concave interior and rounded bottom, interior and exterior slipped orange-red, D: 10 cm; M 712[4] (figure 21).

P. 81, (= object no. 85) disk-shaped saucer/lid, complete vessel, interior and exterior light red/dull orange, D: 9.8 cm; M 712[82].

P.109, two sherds of a disk-shaped saucer/lid, flat-bottomed, red fabric, D: 10.1 cm; M 712[4].

P.110, sherd of a disk-shaped saucer/lid, flat-bottomed, brown fabric, D: 10.2 cm; M 712[17].

P.111, sherd of disk-shaped saucer or lid similar to P.110 but found in M 712[23].

P.113, sherd of a disk-shaped saucer or lid, flat-bottomed, light brown fabric, D: 10.4 cm; M 712[38].

One additional sherd was found in the Amun Temple (context AT 35).

Total frequency count for the saucers/lids was 506% (i.e. at least six vessels) in the M 712 mound and 25%, (one other vessel) in the Amun Temple.

II. Open dishes, plates and plaques

These are shallow, open vessels, although on the basis of rim sherds alone it is sometimes difficult to distinguish between this particular form and large open bowls. Generally speaking, the examples from the Khartoum–Toronto excavations are equivalent to Shinnie and Bradley forms 12-16 and 18-21.

P.128, (= object no. 40) completely preserved small dish with sloping walls, red-washed interior, brown exterior, very coarse brown fabric B, similar to Shinnie and Bradley forms 18 and 19, D: 16 cm; M 712[45] (figure 21).
P.127, flange rim, brown surface, brown fabric (B) with thick carbon streak, D: 26 cm; M 712[38] (figure 21). This form may belong to the same form class as Shinnie and Bradley form 13 and Edwards ZN 756, although our rim sherd is too small to decide this conclusively.
P.112, small rim sherd of a dish or bowl ("flower pot"), fabric B; M 712[39].

One rim sherd of the P.128 type was found at the Amun Temple (AT 35), but while the shape is similar, the fabric is C and there is a painted band on the exterior.

The term "plaque" is used for low flat vessels probably serving as dishes. They tend to be thick, Nile silt fabric presumably Shinnie Ba and Bb and Edwards A2.

P.96, rim sherd, worn surface of a shallow, flat-bottomed plaque, coarse, brown fabric B, D: 31.4 cm; M 712[55], (figure 21).
P.103, shallower than P.96, but generally of the same form and fabric with very dark red slip on the interior; M 712[1].
P.105, similar to P.103; M 712[1].
P.106, similar to P.103; M 712[1].

Total rim count was 117% (i.e. minimum two vessels) for dishes and 39% (i.e. minimum one vessel) for plates/plaques in M 712 and 38% (one vessels) in AT.

III. Doka

Only one sherd of a *doka*, (a vessel used for making *kisra)* has been identified so far. This is somewhat surprising considering the domestic context of our excavations. On the other hand Shinnie and Bradley also list only two examples under their form 137.

P.90, dark brown rim sherd with smoothed surface, coarse black fabric Hc, D: 39 cm; M 712[14] (figure 21).

IV. Large open bowls and jars

Bowls were perhaps the most common type of vessel found on site with the most common being the ubiquitous ledge-rimmed bowls which are separated here somewhat artificially as form class IV. All the other bowls were lumped together as form class III. They vary in size and in some cases the small size of preserved rim fragments made it difficult to determine whether they came from bowls or large open jars. Since most of our examples are known from small rims the identification of specific parallels to Shinnie and Bradley's form classes is a little speculative. However, comparisons could be made with vessels grouped as their forms 17 and 22-33. In terms of fabrics there seem to be a variation, or rather a continuum, ranging from very porous fabric B (e.g. P.98, P.101, P.104), through good quality fabric B (P.130, P.131) as well as the C fabric (P.100, P.102, P.121, P.125-127, P.129).

P.97, large open bowl with slightly ribbed interior, perhaps conical in shape like Shinnie and Bradley form 27 or a footed bowl form 25, brownish-red exterior and interior. The fabric is very coarse B, D: 28.8 cm; M 712[4] (figure 22).

P.98, same form as P.97, light brown fabric B; M 712[1].

P.99, same form and fabric as P.97, but very light brown/creamy exterior slip; M 712[55].

P.100, same form as P.97, but fine fabric C; M 712[1].

P.101, same form and fabric as P.97, but surface red-slipped; M 712[4].

P.102, same form, fabric and colour as P.101; M 712[1].

P.104, same form and fabric as P.97 with red-slipped interior; M 712[14].

P.121, large open bowl, red-slipped exterior, yellowish-brown interior with slight ribbing in the lower part, fabric seems to be coarse C, brown with narrow carbon streak, D: 32.2 cm; M 712[39]-[40] (figure 21). This form shows certain similarity to ZN 707.

P.122, hand-made open bowl, dark exterior, brown interior. Fabric is dark brown to black, very coarse, full of chaff holes and inclusions, H, D: 37.4 cm; M 712[45] (figure 22).

P.123, bowl with an everted rim, thick but good quality light brown/red fabric C, D: 24.8 cm; M 712[14] (figure 22).

P.124, open bowl with vertical, slightly ledged rim, light red exterior and interior slip, light brown fabric C, D: 32.8 cm; M 712[39] (figure 22).

P.125, flanged rim of a large bowl with red slip covering the entire exterior and a thin band inside the vessel; the interior is cream coloured, the fabric is light brown C, D: 44.8 cm; M 712[1] (figure 21), perhaps comparable to Edwards ZN 748 and Shinnie and Bradley form 17.

P.126, straight, flat-topped everted rim slipped light-red on the rim top and in the interior, exterior white slipped with dark red painted decoration (Munsell 7.5 R 4/6), fabric C, D: 31.8 cm; M 712[17] (figure 22).

P.129, medium-thick bowl with orange-red exterior and interior, red-brown fabric C, D: 23 cm; M 712[70] (figure 22).

P.130, small bowl with dark brown exterior, light brown interior, brown fabric B with grey carbon streak, D: 24.2 cm; M 712[2]-[3] (figure 21).

P.131, small bowl with a slight exterior ledge, cream slipped exterior and red-washed interior, fabric B, D: 24.5 cm; M 712[2]-[3] (figure 21).

P.132, small open bowl with exterior groove, red-washed exterior and interior, brown fabric C, D: 18 cm; M 712[39] (figure 22). Comparable example seems to be Musawwarat bowl ZN 727.

P.140, probably the rim of an open jar rather than bowl with exterior grooves and interior ledge, white slipped exterior, dense pink/brown fabric similar to amphora P.139, both being Egyptian imports, presumably Shinnie and Bradley fabric Qa, D: 20.3 cm; M 712[38] (figure 22).

Because the vessels were typically large in diameter the numerous fragments added up to only 132% of the total rim diameter (i.e. a minimum of two vessels.)

V. Ledge-rimmed bowls

The most common late Meroitic bowl type is the ledge-rimmed bowl (plate XXIVa). This is Shinnie and Bradley forms 40-44 and Edwards vessels ZN 732-737, 770, 800. In terms of fabric, they are uniformly described as fabric C in Meroe and fabric B1 at Musawwarat (except for ZN 770 and 800). The Khartoum–Calgary form/pot concordance listed above shows that 24 pots are described as fabric Cc, 18 pots as fabric Cd and 6 pots as fabric Ce. During our excavations the ledge-rimmed bowls were even more common than the saucers/lids and several were found completely preserved. In contrast to previous excavations we have not as yet found footed bowls of Shinnie/Bradley form 42.

P.10, ledge-rimmed, red bowl, complete, rim D: 13.9 cm, H: 9.3 cm; M 712[4] (figure 23).

P.11, ledge-rimmed, red bowl, complete, rim D: 13.2 cm, H: 9.4 cm; M 712[4] (figure 23).

P.13, ledge-rimmed, red bowl with a globular body, complete, rim D: 13.1 cm, H: 9.9 cm; M 712[4] (figure 23).

P.14, ledge-rimmed, red, footed bowl, complete, rim D: 12.2 cm, H: 9.4 cm; M 712[4] (figure 23).

P.15, ledge-rimmed, red-slipped, footed bowl, complete, rim D: 13.6 cm, H: 9.5 cm; M 712[4] (figure 23).

P.16, ledge-rimmed, red-slipped, footed bowl, complete, rim D: 13.5 cm, H: 10 cm; M 712[4] (figure 23).

P.17, ledge-rimmed, red-slipped bowl, complete, D: 14 cm, H: 9.6 cm; M 712[4] (figure 23).

A large quantity of rim sherds were counted but not described. Total rim count amounted to 1731% in M 712 and 80% at the Amun Temple, that is a minimum of 19 vessels. *Context 4*, alone, accounted for all the complete vessels and another 187% of rim sherds.

Two bowls have ledge rim but round base and/or represent different fabric:

P.1, (=object no.12) everted rim, carinated body and round bottom, red slipped exterior and interior, pink fabric with numerous straw inclusions, rim D: 12.3 cm, H: 8.6 cm; M 712[9] (figure 23). The shape is identical to Shinnie and

Bradley form 58, except that their example was black and handmade.

P.63, also had a ledge rim, but clearly represents a different form if only because of the size difference. Its exterior and interior have pink slip and the exterior is decorated with a painted band of dark pink/light red colour, glued from two sherds, fabric is presumably Cc, D: 19.9 cm; M 712[55] (figure 23).

VI. Fine ware bowls and cups

The Meroitic fine wares, or egg-shell wares, are usually treated, and rightly so, as a separated category by all the authors. In terms of form, they comprise two kinds of vessels, namely small very fine thin-walled bowls and cups, often decorated with incised and/or painted designs. Shinnie and Bradley distinguished three sub-groups: Fa - comprising unslipped white ware with painted decoration; Fb - with stamped or painted and stamped decoration; Fc - bright red, highly polished exterior slip with interior occasionally showing painted decoration. Since these vessels represent such an exceptionally important class where the decoration, rather than the vessel shape is the key element of the chronological and comparative studies, the decorated body sherds were included in the sherd catalogue.

P.5, rim sherd of a fine cup or bowl with inward-sloping neck and painted decoration around the rim, fabric Fa, D: 7 cm; M 712[45] (figure 29).

P.31, fine egg-shell bowl with pink-coloured body 5YR 7/3, red-painted rim line 10R 4/6-4/8 and stamped decoration on the exterior somewhat similar to Edwards ZN 314. The motif is unclear, perhaps a tadpole, D: 13.9 cm; M 712[74] (figure 24).

P.32 and **P.32a**, fine, white ware cup decorated with ankhs outlined in brown/maroon painted with the red paint inside the *ankhs* applied in blotches and not as a careful infill of the design, paint 5YR 3/2, slip 10YR 8/3, interior 10YR 8/2, D: 10 cm; rim found in M 712[45] (figure 24), body sherd from M 712[74] (figure 24).

P.33, stamped body sherd with a quatrefoil or truncated *ankh* design, white slip 7.5YR 8/2; M 712[74] (figure 25).

P.34, stamped sherd with *ankh* motif, white slip, similar to P.33; M 712[6] (figure 25).

P.35, stamped sherd with frogs, like Shinnie and Bradley fig.56a, but dark red slip 10R 4/6, unusual black, soft fabric, probably Nile silt (A2?); M 712[39] (figure 25).

P.36, stamped sherd with painted lines, design reddish yellow 5YR 6/6, lines dark red/brown 10R 3/4, body off-white; M 712[39] (figure 25).

P.37, stamped rim, off-white, lozenges motif similar to Shinnie and Bradley, fig. 57c; M 712[39] (figure 24).

P.38, stamped cream white body and base sherd similar to P.37; M 712[38].

P.39, stamped rim sherd, very worn but originally red-slipped, with ear (*mesedjer*) motif (see Török 1997a:Fig.98 No.108), D: 14 cm; M 712[77] (figure 24).

P.40, stamped rim sherd, cream white slip, red painted lines, D: 14.9 cm; M 712[38] (figure 24).

P.41, stamped rim sherd probably from a cup, white slip, light red lines 7.5YR 5/8 near the rim, dark red 7.5YR 2.5/4 below, D: 11.8 cm; M 712[45] (figure 24).

P.42, rim sherd stamped slip white, lines painted brown-red 7.5YR 2.5/4, painted interior, D: 9.9 cm; M 712[23] (figure 24).

P.43, small rim sherd stamped with the bees motif, a variant of Shinnie and Bradley fig. 53c, cream white slip, black/brown painted lines 2.5YR 3/2, D: 13.4 cm; M 712[45] (figure 24).

P.44, glued from three painted body sherds and part of the base, exterior slip white 10YR 8/3, interior white 5YR 8/2, painted decoration of successive altars and long-stemmed *ankhs*; outlines drawn in brown/dark-red paint 5YR 3/3, infill 10R 6/8-4/8, two brown/dark red lines around the base, fabric fine clay but with sand and grog impurities; compare with Shinnie and Bradley fig. 50c, Garstang 1911:44 and Pl.XLVII, Török 1997: Pl.223; M712[45] (figure 25; plate XXIVd).

P.45, body sherd painted with orange lines, slip creamy-pink exterior, white interior; M 712[45] (figure 25).

P.46, body sherd, exterior paint dark-brown lines, dark-orange fill, see Shinnie and Bradley fig. 49g; M 712[45] (figure 25).

P.47, body sherd with white/pinkish exterior, painted dark red/brown lines, buff interior; M 712[45] (figure 25).

P.48, body sherd, exterior painted large red dot, brown/black horizontal lines, two brown lines painted on the interior; M 712[45] (figure 25).

P.49, body sherd, white-yellow slip, brown lines; M 712[39]-[40] (figure 25).

P.50, body sherd, exterior orange-yellow slip, brown painted *ankhs*; M 712[39] (figure 25).

P.51, body sherd, dirty white/grey slip, brown painted lines; M 712[2]-[3] (figure 25).

P.52, body sherd, white slip, orange/ brown lines; M 712[45] (figure 25).

P.53, body sherd, white slip, brown painted lines; M 712[39]-[40] (figure 25).

P.54, bowl rim sherd, bright red exterior slip 10R 6/8 (ware Fc), dusty red/brown painted lines, D: 21 cm; M 712[45] (figure 24).

P.55, body sherd, exterior red slip same as P.54, *ankh* painted brown/black, interior white slip; M 712[45] (figure 25).

P.56, body sherd, white slipped exterior and interior (ware Fa), interior painted brown vine leaf, interior painted black dots and brown lines; M 712[45] (figure 25).

P.57, bowl rim sherd, red slipped exterior 10R 6/8 (ware Fc), white interior painted with brown horizontal lines and dark brown dot, D: 17.8 cm; M 712[45] (figure 24).

P.58, bowl rim sherd, red slipped exterior same as P.57, light interior with burgundy/brown lines and yellow-brown infill, D: 18 cm; M 712[55] (figure 24).

P.59, large rim sherd from a bowl, red-slipped exterior same as P.57, white-slipped interior, brown lines, triangle filled red, D: 18 cm; M 712, context not recorded, (figure 24).

P.60, four sherds from a bowl, red slip exterior 10R 5/8, interior white 10YR 8/3 decorated with straight brown lines 5YR 3/2 along the rim and red *ankhs* 2.5YR 5/8 outlined in brown, D: 19.8 cm; M 712[45] (figure 24).

P.61, fine ware cup or goblet, or neck of a beer jar, white slipped exterior with alternating brown and red lines 7.5R 5/8, light pink interior 5YR 7/4, D: 12.1 cm; M 712, context not recorded (figure 29).

P.79, bowl rim sherd, red slipped exterior 7.5R 5/8, stamped with two lines of the *heker* motif separated by black painted lines, D: 20.8 cm; M 712[82] (figure 25).

P.80, body sherd with cream-coloured exterior slip 7.5YR 8/4, white slip in the interior 10YR 8/3, exterior painted dark brown and red; M 712[82] (figure 25).

P.83, small sherd with the *ankh* on the crescent design; M 712[70] (figure 25).

P.143, thin-walled, finely polished glossy red slipped exterior and interior 7.5R 5/8, typical example of the Fc fabric, D: 14.8 cm; M 712, context not recorded (figure 24; plate XXIVf).

P.144, same as P. 143 but larger, D: 17.8 cm; M 712, context not recorded (figure 24; plate XXIVf).

P.145, medium-thick bowl, white slipped interior and top lip of the rim, matte red exterior with thin parallel grooves, fabric uncertain, D: 25.5 cm; M 712, context not recorded (figure 25).

P.146, red-slipped cup similar in fabric to P.143 and P.144, D: 8 cm; M 712[4] (figure 29).

The total number of egg-shell ware sherds was 119, including 19 sherds with stamped decoration, 37 sherds with painted exterior (plate XXIVb), 19 sherds with painted interior (plate XXIVc; exterior always red-slipped) and 35 undecorated sherds. This group contained two sherds with stamped exterior and painted interior, one sherd painted externally, with a single painted line painted on the interior and one sherd (P.56) painted on both sides. Edwards (1999d:28) recorded 420 stamped sherds representing 1.32% of the total number of sherds. In Meroe, the 19 stamped sherds represented 0.6% of the total sherd number. In terms of rim percentages there were a minimum of four vessels (305%) found at M 712 and one (5%) at the Amun Temple belonging to the fabric types Fa and Fb. As for the Fc fabric, the rim count was 336% in M 712 and 111% in the Amun Temple, i.e. a minimum of four and two vessels respectively. It is noticeable that a substantial number of these fine ware vessels was associated with just two contexts, M 712[79] and M 712[45].

VII. Large hand-made black ware bowls and jars

Although the form is similar to other bowls, these are grouped separately because the vessels are all black and hand-made (plate XXVa-c). They are the equivalent of Shinnie and Bradley fabric K. The examples given by these authors are almost exclusively open bowls for drinking (e.g. form 24, P.118, and form 35, P.198) or storing and cooking (e.g. form 87, P.200 and form 85, P.213). Our list includes the following forms: open bowls (e.g. P.69-72, P.76), straight-walled bowls or cups (e.g. P.78), slightly constricted, carinated bowls (e.g. P.65) and constricted (inverted) bowls (e.g. P.67, P.74, P.77). The hand-made black bottles like P.67, P.75 perhaps also ought to be incorporated here, although presently they are included in a separate category (see below).

P.65, similar form to red ware bowl P.1, but longer body narrowing towards the rim and more pronounced carination, exterior and interior are black, fabric brown, more likely Ja rather than Kb of Shinnie and Bradley pot 345 (form 58), D: 12.1 cm; M 712[2]-[3] (figure 23).

P.67, bowl with incurving upper body, hand-made but very smooth, jet-black exterior in its lower part rouletted decoration with traces of red pigment, grey-black interior with rouletted decoration on the inside rim ledge, rim D: 25.8 cm; M 712[38] (figure 26).

P.68, black body sherd, fabric Kc, with the exterior rouletted decoration originally filled with white pigment and depicting an animal, perhaps an elephant or a cow, comparable to Shinnie and Bradley Fig. 58c; M 712[14] (figure 28).

P.69, rim and body sherd of dark grey/black vessel, exterior with rouletted

decoration of large triangles, D: 32.8 cm; M 712[39] (figure 26; plate XXVa).

P.70, black burnished bowl with an incised band of cris-crossed lines 1 cm below the rim, D: 32 cm; M 712[39]-[40] (figure 26; plate XXVb).

P.71, open bowl with straight-sided thick rim and incised linear decoration of the exterior, perhaps Neolithic (?), D: 32 cm; M 712[39] (figure 26; plate XXVc).

P.72, open bowl with rows of diagonally placed rouletted decoration, D: 30.2 cm; M 712[6] (figure 26).

P.73, incurved bowl rim sherd, rouletted decoration, fabric Kc, rim D: 27.8 cm; M 712[39] (figure 26).

P.74, small incurved bowl with incised decoration along the rim edge and rim exterior, D: 17.9 cm; M 712[1] (figure 26; plate XXVc).

P.76, two sherds from large open bowl with a band of rouletted horizontal and vertical lines in the upper part of the vessel, fabric Kc or Kd, D: 31.6 cm; M 712[1], M 712[45] (figure 26).

P.77, rim and handle sherd of a small (beer?) jar with constricted mouth, rim D: 7 cm; M 712[11] (figure 28).

P.78, sherd of a thin jar with constricted mouth found embedded into a wall, rim D: 11.9 cm; M 712[11] (figure 28).

The total rim sherds count of the hand-made black wares amounts to 293% (i.e. a minimum of three vessels). If bottles P.66 and P.75 were to be included the total rim percentage would be 378%.

Another problematic group provisionally included in the black wares class category comprises five small sherds of hand-made vessels of brown rather than black fabric. They seem to come from small bowls or cups. Rim percentage: 20%.

P.82, a small and unusual looking sherd with rows of short horizontal incisions on the exterior and additional incision on the lip of the rim, exterior dark grey/black 5YR 4/1, interior reddish-brown 5 YR 5/4, perhaps Neolithic, rim D: 9 cm; M 712[17] (figure 28).

P.133, rim and body sherd, thin, brown with rouletted decoration, fabric similar to P.82; M 712[70].

P.134, rim sherd similar to P.133; M 712[55].

VIII. Amphorae

Since the amphorae are usually used for the shipping and storing of liquids, they tend to include a higher proportion of imported vessels. They can be easily recognized in the pottery assemblage due to their small rim diameter, handles and, more often than not, elongated necks. Also, many amphorae can be identified because of their characteristic bases.

P.7, (= object no. 70) found broken but reconstructible, although with many body sherds missing, fabric is brown 7.5YR 6/6, that is Shinnie and Bradley B type, probably Bd, the vessel is long with a button base, ribbing in the interior, rim D: 7.5 cm, maximum D: 11 cm, H: 33 cm; it was found together with potstand P.8 in M 712[4] (figure 27; plate XXVe).

P.19, lower part of a large amphora with ribbed black/grey interior, exterior red, narrowing towards base; AT 37 (figure 30).

P.139, neck and handle stem of an imported Egyptian amphora of good quality pink/brown fabric, presumably Shinnie and Bradley Qa, exterior pinkish/cream, 5YR 7/5-7/8, double handles, ribbing in the rim interior, rim D: 10 cm; M 712[1] (figure 27).

P.141, amphora neck and handle, red fabric, green wash 2.5Y 8/2-8/4, Egyptian Qena ware, rim D: 5.4 cm; M 712[6] (figure 27).

P.148, round bottomed base, brown/black fabric, orange exterior and interior; AT 35 (figure 27).

P.150, red-slipped brown fabric with carbon streak and button base; M 712[45] (figure 27).

P.151, stemmed, flat-footed base of an amphora or a goblet, fabric is black/grey, surface white but with green spots, both fabric and surface are similar to amphora P.7 and beer jar P.116; M 712[55] (figure 27).

The minimum number of vessels based on the rim percentage count is 350%, that is four amphorae. Four more handles were also found: one in M 712[75] and one from M 712[8], the provenance of the others two has not been recorded. This would suggest the presence of two more vessels.

IX. Cups and beakers

Only one vessel presently represents this group, which comprises the so-called "feeding cups" and small cups and bowls made in fabrics other than F.

P.135, large fragment of a small bowl or cup similar to Shinnie and Bradley form 7 "baby feeding bottle" but without a spout, brown fabric, brown exterior, traces of white wash in the interior, D: 5.9 cm; M 712[39] (figure 28).

X. Bottles and necked jars

This category includes vessels identified mainly on the basis of long, straight or inward-sloping rim sherds presumably from the long-necked jars and bottles so well known from Gabati (see Rose 1998:147-157). These are equivalent of Shinnie and Bradley forms 113-116 and perhaps also forms 96 and 97 as well as

Edwards ZN 712, ZN 772 and the like. Some of the vessels presently included in this group may in fact represent a different category (P.61, P.66, P.75).

P.62, outflaring rim, white exterior and interior, alternating brown/black lines and red bands, presumably fabric Ce, rim D: 15 cm; M 712[45] (figure 29; plate XXVd).

P.64, modelled rim and neck sherd, creamy pink exterior with painted black band, interior pinkish, white and red painted below the rim, fabric C, very similar to Edwards ZN 771, rim D: 10 cm; M 712[45] or [55] (figure 29; plate XXVd).

P.66, either a modelled neck or part of a small jar, black fabric similar to Ka but wheel-made, burnished, rim top decorated with chevrons, rim D: 9.7 cm; M 712[2]-[3] (figure 29).

P.75, thin-walled bottle neck with grooves, rim D: 8.9 cm; M 712, context not recorded (figure 29).

P.114, long beer jar neck, red/orange exterior 10R 5/8, orange/brown interior 5YR 6/6 with ribbing, fabric C, rim D: 8 cm; M 712[4] (figure 29).

P.115, long beer jar neck, light red exterior and interior, fabric C, rim D: 10.2 cm; M 712[17] (figure 29).

P.116, short-necked beer jar fabric Bb, exterior red slipped 10R 5/6, interior light brown 7.5YR 6/6; M 712[8].

P.117, short-necked beer jar, hand-made, similar to Shinnie and Bradley form 94, Edwards ZN 804, red-brown fabric Hc, light brown exterior wash, soot-covered; M 712[8].

P.118, long-necked beer jar, similar to P.114.

P.136, bottle rim sherd, red/brown fabric, white slip exterior and interior, rim D: 10.3 cm; M 712[6] (figure 29).

P.137, small sherd of a small brown ware bottle, fabric and appearance similar to P.82, seems to be fabric B, rim D: 8 cm; M 712, context not recorded (figure 29).

P.138, small, flat-topped bottle rim, bright red exterior, brown fabric, rim D: 8.3 cm; M 712[82] (figure 29).

P.142, either an incurving long neck of a bottle or top part of a goblet, fabric brown, red-slipped exterior, red/brown wash interior, rim D: 9 cm; M 712[55] (figure 29).

P.147, either a long, outward-sloping bottle neck or top part of a goblet, brown fabric C, exterior dark red, interior red, rim D: 14.4 cm; AT 35 (figure 29).

In terms of form and function the previously discussed black-ware, hand-made, simple-rimmed beer jars P.77 and P.78 belong in fact to this class. Another vessels that could also be provisionally included here, due to its narrow mouth, is P.119. Finally, sherd P.61 (figure 29), already discussed as class VI fine ware cup or goblet, may have been in fact a fragment of a long-necked jar. Another problematic vessel is P. 119:

P.119, constricted small bowl or jar, pinkish-red exterior and interior, fabric B, rim D: 11.9 cm; M 712[2]-[3] (figure 28).

The total rim sherd count, excluding pots P.77, P.78 and P.119, amounted to 405% (five vessels) in M 712 and 128% (two vessels) in the Amun Temple.

XI. Goblets

This form is very difficult to identify from sherds alone. It has been suggested above that P.147 might in fact be a goblet. Perhaps the heavy, flat-bottomed bases, like P.149, could be identified as goblets, similar to Shinnie and Bradley forms P.62 and P.63. Base P.151 could have come from a goblet or an amphora.

P.149, heavy, flat base with slight ribbing in the interior, light brown fabric, spotted dirty-white exterior, yellow/brown interior; M 712[39] (figure 27).

The total percentage of heavy flat bases amounted to 300% in M 712 and 400% in AT 35, suggesting at least seven vessels. Whether these bases were part of goblets or footed bowls or even amphorae is impossible to determine.

XII. Tashit

Fragments of three different basins (Arabic *tashit*) were found in AT 35. They all have low, straight walls and had square or rectangular shape (plate XIIId). Perhaps these were offering basins rather than domestic basins.

XIII. Bread moulds

Bread moulds are commonly associated with palace and temple bakeries. During our excavations one bread mould and one bread mould sherd were found at M 712. Six fragments of four bread moulds were found in AT 35.

P.88, bottom of a bread mould, preserved height 7 cm; M 712[39]-[55] (figure 27).
P.89, small tip of a bread mould; M 712[2]-[3].

XIV. Footed stands

This is Shinnie and Bradley's rare form 135 and called by them "candlestick," presumably on account of the shape rather than function. Edwards (1999d:26) calls them offering stands, e.g. ZN 778, and Rose (1999:145) uses the term "footed stands." These vessels are formed by two cup-like containers joined by a stem. When found incomplete it is

difficult to identify the base part, although the sloping cavity in the stem may suggest that this was the base. Our illustration of a footed stand P.9 is probably placed upside-down (figure 30; plate XIIIc). Although charcoal was associated with P.2, neither in this vessel nor in P.9 were there any obvious fire stains or soot remains. Apparently no traces of burning were recognized in the Gabati examples either and therefore one should entertain the possibility that these vessels served as chalices for libation rather than as incense burners, which tend to be heavier and less finely executed. One example that seems to represent a brazier or an incense burner is P.18.

P.2, (=object no. 13) tulip-shaped cup with everted rim, either base or top of the footed stand, light red, rim D: 9.2 cm; M 712[9] (figure 30).
P.9, stem and cup or base of a footed stand, light red; AT 35 (figure 30; plate XIIIc).
P.18, stem and cup fragment, very heavy, but good quality pink fabric; M 712[55] (figure 30).
P.28, thick stem fragment, possibly from a footed stand, red-brown crust-covered exterior, yellow-brown interior, D: 7.6 cm; M 712[24] (figure 28).
P.29, stem fragment similar to P.28, D: 7.2 cm; M 712[2]-[3].
P.30, stem fragment similar to P.28, D: 8.9 cm; M 712[11].

XV. Pipes

Pipes have been previously found by Shinnie and Bradley, pot form 132. So far only one ceramic object found by the Khartoum–Toronto mission can be identified as a pipe.

P.20, long section of a thick ceramic pipe with undulating exterior surface and ribbed interior, red, D: 21 cm; M 712[55]-[38] (figure 28).

XVI. Potstands

Unless found complete these cannot be distinguished from jar rims. Only one complete potstand has been found and it was uncovered together with its companion piece, amphora P.7.

P.8, (= object no. 69) potstand with open interior and outcurving rims, brown fabric similar to P.7, base D: 12.1 cm, rim D: 9.7 cm, H: 7.7 cm; M 712[4] (figure 27; plate XXVe).

XVII. Diskettes

Several large, re-used, disk-shaped sherds with smoothed edges were noticed. Some might have served for digging, but the majority were probably used as lids. Their diameter varies from 3.5 to 6 cm.

P.21, sherd of a large, red-slipped jar, with brown/grey interior, smoothed edges, coarse fabric, D: 9.5 cm; M 712[55] (figure 30).
P.22, sherd similar to P.21 but smaller, coarse fabric, D: 3.5 cm; M 712[30] (figure 30).
P.23, sherd similar to P.21, D: 5.2 cm; M 712[39]-[40] (figure 30).
P.24, sherd similar to P.21 but exterior orange/red, coarse fabric, D: 6.2-7.2 cm; M 712[14] (figure 30).
P.25, sherd similar to P.24, coarse fabric, D: 6.2 cm; M 712[14].
P.26, sherd similar to P.22, exterior red-brown, interior light red, good clay-silt mix fabric, D: 4 cm; M 712[2]-[3].
P.27, jar sherd, dark red/plum exterior slip, red/brown interior, medium coarse fabric, D: 3.5 cm; M 712[39]-[40].

XVIII. Miscellaneous

Three fragments of Eastern *sigillata*, or their Aswan imitation, vessels were found on mound M 712. No attempts at dating have been made yet.

P.85, fragment of a small (cosmetic?) vessel, exterior glossy red 10R 5/8, interior ranges from red/pink 7.5R 6/8 to yellowish/cream 7.5YR 8/4, fabric orange-pink 5YR 6/8, shoulder D: 10 cm; M 712[39]-[55] (figure 25).
P.86, sherd similar to P.85, but matte; M 712, no context recorded.
P.87, base fragment, colours and fabric as P.85, base D: 8 cm; M 712[30] (figure 25).
P.91, Eastern sigillata base fragment, glossy red exterior, similar to P.85-87; M 712[38].
P.92, Eastern sigillata sherd, glossy red exterior and interior, similar to P.85-87; M 712[39].

THE SMALL FINDS

Considering the domestic nature of the excavated unit the objects found in M 712, and even in the Amun Temple, are predominantly utilitarian and not very impressive. The organic material, like basketry or cloth, has not survived except for the burnt remains of what seemed to have been a *tabak* (a basketry tray cover), found in context M 712[4]. The majority of the surviving artefacts were made of stone and include a large number of querns, grinding stones and pounders, although a few faience beads and iron pieces were also found. The finds were numbered consecutively in the order of recording.

I. Stone objects

The majority of stone objects were various kinds of grinding stones, querns

POTTERY AND SMALL FINDS

and palettes. The latter ones are characterized by a flat surface on one side and slightly convex surface on the other side. When first found they were assumed to have served as palettes for grinding minerals, cosmetics and other such items. However, the discovery of a palette (no.73) in association with large millstone (no.72) would suggest that the palettes were used as grinding stones as well.

1. A piece of hard brown stone, perhaps large river chert pebble, smooth on both surfaces, with sharp and pointy broken edges. It is unclear whether it is a fragment of a statue or simply a naturally smoothed large pebble. L: 13.9 cm, maximum thickness: 7.2 cm; AT 5.
3. Sandstone grinder, round with circular use/wear patterns, 4.5 x 3.7 cm; AT 5 (plate XXVc).
4. Round sandstone object assembled from two pieces with a 3 cm wide hole in the middle and an elongated incision along one surface, identified as a loom weight by our workmen but might have been a small millstone, D: 16 cm, Th: 5 cm; M 712[17] (figure 41; plate XXVIa).
5. Fragment of a granite saddle quern broken in the thin, middle part, 13.5 x 12.5 x 3-6 cm; M 712[17].
6. Round but irregular pounder or grinding stone with one flat surface, 8.3 x 7.7 cm; M 712[17] (plate XXVIc).
7. Irregularly shaped grinding stone with smooth, almost flat surface, 11.7 cm x 6.7 cm; M 712[17].
8. Buff coloured, thin sandstone palette, smooth on one side, slightly convex on other side, 10.5 x 2.20 cm; M 712[17] (plate XXVId).
9. Slightly concave sandstone quern fragment, broken in the thin middle part, preserved L: 9.5 cm, W: 11.5 cm, Th: 1.8 cm; M 712[17] (plate XXVId).

10. Rectangular palette with rounded corners, 11.6 x 8.5 x 2.7 cm; M 712[17] (plate XXVId).
11. Oval shaped hard (granite?) stone saddle quern with a convex surface, 21.5 x 11.4 x 5.8 cm; M 712[17].
14. Pounder with flat bottom surface smoothed from wear, 5.9 x 4.2 cm; M 712[2]-[3] (plate XXVIc).
15. Buff coloured grinding stone with circular use pattern, 5.1 x 4.8 cm; M 712[2]-[3] (plate XXVIc).
16. Hammerstone with a small circular depression, probably used also as grinding tool because of the smoothed, but salt-covered top surface, 4.2 x 3.3 cm; M 712[2]-[3] (plate XXVIc).
17. Flat and squarish stone probably used as grinding tool, 4.4 x 3.9 x 2.1 cm; M 712[2]-[3] (plate XXVIc).
18. Circular grinding stone, partly broken, 5.8 x 5.1 x 2.1 cm; M 712[2]-[3] (plate XXVIc).
19. Small quern fragment L: 5.9 cm, Th: 2.4 cm; M 712[2]-[3] (plate XXVId).
20. Ovoid palette or grinding stone, one surface smooth, other surface rough, 12.2 x 9 x 3.7 cm; M 712[2]-[3] (plate XXVId).
22. Ovoid palette of dark sandstone, one side very smooth, other rough, very worn in the centre, 10.2 x 8.1 x 2 cm; M 712[14].
23. Pounder with two flat surfaces, 5.4 x 4.5 cm; M 712[7] (figure 41; plate XXVIc).
24. Pounder, very worn and chipped off, 4.1 x 3.9 cm; M 712[10].
25. Fragment of sandstone quern or large palette with one surface convex, and one edge broken off, 19 x 13 x 3.1 cm; M 712[10].
26. Circular grinding stone with one side smooth the other probably used as pounder, D: 7 cm, Th: 3 cm; M 712[10].

71

29. Polishing stone, oval, yellowish quartzite pebble, slightly chipped at both ends, 4.8 x 2.6 cm; M 712[10].

30. Polishing stone, oval yellowish quartzite pebble, with both narrow ends showing wear pattern suggest perhaps use in burnishing pottery, 6.6 x 5.9 x 4.2 cm; M 712[10] (plate XVIIb, second row, left).

31. Pounder, heavily worn, almost cubic in appearance with three concave surfaces, D: 6.1 cm, Th: 4.2 cm; M 712[10].

32. Whetstone, elongated, brown, highly polished pebble chert, 8.5 x 3.8 x 2.4 cm; M 712[10].

33. Piece of rectangular pink stone, very porous, slightly concave one top surface, perhaps a quern or a large pounder, 11.8 x 8.5 x 4.3 cm; M 712[10] (plate XVIIb, top row, left).

34. Yellow sandstone fragment, perhaps a palette, roughly triangular with one surface rough, other surface smooth but with two oval incisions giving it an appearance of a face L: 13.8, maximum W: 9.3 cm, Th: 4.1 cm; M 712[10] (plate XVIIb top row, centre).

35. Half of a red sandstone quern or palette, flat on one side, convex on the other side, 11.5 x 12.5 cm; M 712[10] (plate XVIIb, top row, right).

36. Banded agate probably used for burnishing or polishing, 4.1. x 3.9 1.9 cm; M 712[10].

39. Black coloured, round bead, D: 5 mm; AT 28.

41. Oval-shaped white sandstone palette with small chips on the edges, 9.7 x 8.3 x 2.1 cm; M 712[39] (plate XXVId).

42. Ovoid-shaped grey sandstone palette, with one surface slightly concave, 13.9 x 11.1 x 2.3 cm; M 712[39] (plate XXVId).

43. Pounder, very heavy, with traces of iron and rust, a groove running around the stone presumably for tying it or siding into a forked handle, D: 5.7 cm, Th: 3.5 cm; M 712[39].

44. Elongated fragment of a saddle quern broken off at the thin end, densely covered with salt incrustation, porous, white sandstone, preserved L: 17 cm, W: 8.7 cm, Th: 4.4 cm; M 712[45].

45. Large, brown chert pebble used as a pounder as indicated by a worn and weathered side, 6.2 x 5.4 x 4.6 cm; M 712[17] (plate XXVIc).

46. Round, quartzite polishing stone, chipped off at one end, D: 4.6 cm, Th: 2.2 cm; M 712[23].

47. Flat piece of stone with slight concavity covered with salt grains, 14.3 x 9.6 x 3.5 cm; M 712[23] (plate XXVId).

60. Very finely made quartzite arrowhead, complete, except for a tiny bit of the tip, slightly serrated edges, L: 2.1 cm, W: 0.8 cm, Th: 0.4 cm; M 712[39] (figure 41).

61. Small, thin, white ring bead, identified as stone due to hardness, D: 5 mm, Th: 1 mm; M 712[30].

63. Broken quartzite pounder or hammerstone, 5.1 x 3.7 x 3.7 cm; AT 28.

68. Elongated, dark quartzite pebble with both narrow ends worked out, one with rounded dull surface, the other sharp-edged, L: 5.4 cm, W: 4.1 cm, Th: 2.7 cm; M 712[24].

72. Millstone, very large rectangular quern with slightly rounded edges and concavity placed a little off-centre, the stone is yellow-grey, soft and very brittle, cracked in several places, found together with a grinding stone/palette, field no.73 (below), 37 x 34 x 9 cm; M 712[3] (unit 2) (plate XXVIb).

73. Palette-like grinding stone, slightly convex on one side, flat on the other side, traces of wear on both side, found next to, but below millstone field no.72, D: 12 cm, Th: 2 cm; M 712[3] (unit 2) (plate XXVIb).

84. Oval shaped, dark ironstone hammerstone, smooth, but with marks on one end, 5.9 x 5.3 x 4.4 cm; M 712[39] (figure 41).

86. Round piece of yellow sandstone with a hole in the middle, uneven thickness, presumably a spindle whorl, D: 3.4 cm, Th: 0.9-1.4 cm; M 712[75] (figure 41).

II. Faience objects

37. Cylindrical faience bead, faintly turquoise colour, L: 3.5 mm, Th: 3 mm; AT 26.

38. Long, cylindrical faience bead, L: 21 mm, Th: 2.5 mm; AT 27.

55. Corner fragment of a faience tile with red fabric and bright green exterior, 6.5 x 5.8 x 1.5 cm; M 712[55].

57. Round, ball-shaped bead of white material, probably faience, D: 6 mm, Th: 5 mm; M 712[32].

58. Large, round, ring-shaped bead with incised decoration of parallel lines on outside surface, very large hole, D: 17 mm, Th: 13.5 mm, hole D: 7.5 mm; M 712[29] (figure 43).

62. Small, cylindrical bead, D: 3 mm, Th: 2 mm; AT 28 (figure 43)

64. Unidentifiable, shapeless piece of faience, but with noticeable corner, perhaps from a plaque, 2.4 x 1.3 cm; AT 39.

67. Elongated tubular bead of buff-grey colour, possibly made of faience, L: 12 mm, D: 0.4 mm; M 712[7] or [17].

87. Faience plaque, yellow-range fabric, light green exterior, decoration impressed, only the top part of the knot-design preserved, design and frame in high relief, back smooth, edges rounded, preserved L: 5.2 cm, W: 4.2 cm, Th: 1.9 cm; M 712 [59] (figure 43; plate XXVIf).

III. Metal objects

2. Small, roundish lump of copper, perhaps a bead, 6 mm; AT 5.

21. Copper nail, corroded, rounded, slightly uneven shank, irregular head, wider on one side, L: 2.4 cm, stem Th: 0.55 cm, head Th: 0.7 cm; M 712[2]-[3].

50. Shiny piece of what seems to be molten glass or metal, or maybe a mineral, perhaps galena (?), 1 x 0.5 cm; M 712[16].

51. A tiny piece of metal foil, gold-coloured on one side, grey on the other side, 1 x 0.1 cm; M 712[4].

52. Elongated leaf-shaped iron arrowhead with rounded shoulders and long thin tang, broken into two pieces, the lower half shows remains of the wooden shaft still attached to the tang, very corroded, but otherwise well preserved; found together with nos. 53 and 54, L: 6.3 cm (arrowhead), 3.6 cm (tang), W: 2 cm (arrowhead), 0.8 cm (tang), Th: 0.75 cm; M 712[55] (figure 42; plate XXVIe).

53. Top part of iron arrowhead of a narrow, elongated type, base broken off, corroded, found together with nos. 52 and 54, preserved L: 4.7 cm, W: 1.2 cm, Th: 0.55 cm; M 712[55] (figure 42; plate XXVIe).

54. Two large and three small pieces presumably from arrowhead(s), L: 1 to 3 cm; M 712[55].

56. Tanged, iron arrowhead, corroded, preserved L: 3 cm, W: 1.5 cm, Th: 0.6 cm; M 712[70] (figure 42; plate XXVIe).

59. Unidentified curving iron object, perhaps a hook or bracelet or a horse bit fragment, very corroded, broken into several pieces, L: 6.7 cm, W: 1.2 cm, Th: 0.8 cm; M 712[38].

65. Corroded, and therefore misshapen iron nail, H: 6.2 cm total, 1.2 cm head, W: 0.4 cm base, 1.6 cm head; AT 49 (figure 42).

66. Three corroded pieces of iron nail or wire, D: 3 mm, L: 14 mm, 17 mm, 18 mm; M 712[45].

74. Leaf-shaped iron arrowhead, corroded, L: 4.6 cm, W: 1.8 cm, Th: 0.45 cm; M 712[38] (figure 42; plate XXVIe).

75. Thin, long iron arrowhead or perhaps nail, very corroded, D: 0.6 cm, L: 7.2 cm; M 712[4] (figure 42; plate XXVIe).

Register of Small Finds

1. Stone piece AT 5
2. Green bead(?) AT 5
3. Sandstone grinder AT 5
4. Loom weight M 712[17]
5. Quern fragment M 712[17]
6. Pounder/grinder M 712[17]
7. Grinder M 712[17]
8. Palette M 712[17]
9. Quern M 712[17]
10. Palette M 712[17]
11. Grinding stone M 712[17]
12. Bowl M 712[9] = pot P.1
13. "Candlestick" M 712[9] = pot P.2
14. Pounder M 712[2]-[3]
15. Grinder M 712 [2]-[3]
16. Hammerstone/grinder M 712[2]-[3]
17. Grinder M 712[2]-[3]
18. Grinder M 712[2]-[3]
19. Quern fragment M 712[2]-[3]
20. Grinding stone M 712[2]-[3]
21. Nail M 712[2]-[3]
22. Palette M 712[14]
23. Pounder M 712[7]
24. Pounder M 712[10]
25. Quern M 712[10]
26. Grinder M 712[10]
27. Clay dish M 712[10] = pot P.3
28. Clay dish M 712[10] = pot P.4
29. Polishing stone M 712[10]
30. Polishing stone M 712[10]
31. Pounder M 712[10]
32. Whetstone M 712[10]
33. Quern (?) M 712[10]
34. Decorated palette M 712[10]
35. Quern or palette M 712[10]
36. Hammerstone M 712[10]
37. Bead AT 26
38. Bead AT 27
39. Bead AT 28
40. Clay dish M 712[45] = pot P.5
41. Quern M 712[39]
42. Quern M 712[39]
43. Pounder M 712[39]
44. Quern M 712[45]
45. Pounder M 712[17]
46. Polishing stone M 712[23]
47. Quern M 712[23]
48. Saucer/lid M 712[17] = pot P.6
49. Saucer/lid M 712[11] = pot P.7
50. Mineral M 712[16]
51. Yellow foil M 712[4]
52. Arrowhead M 712[55]
53. Arrowhead M 712[55]
54. Iron pieces M 712[55]
55. Tile fragment M 712[55]
56. Arrowhead M 712[70]
57. Bead M 712[32}
58. Bead M 712[29]
59. Iron object M 712[38]
60. Quartzite arrowhead M 712[39]
61. Bead M 712[30]
62. Bead AT 28
63. Hammerstone AT 28
64. Faience fragment AT 39
65. Nail AT 49
66. Iron pieces M 712[45]
67. Bead M 712[17]
68. Hammerstone M 712[24]
69. Potstand M 712[4] = pot P.8
70. Amphora M 712[4] = pot P.7
71. "Candlestick" AT 35 = pot P.9
72. Millstone M 712[3], unit 2
73. Palette M 712[3], unit 2
74. Arrowhead M 712[38]
75. Arrowhead or nail M 712[4]
76. Clay bowl M 712[4] = pot P.10
77. Clay bowl M 712[4] = pot P.11
78. Saucer/lid M 712[4] = pot P.12
79. Clay bowl M 712[4] = pot P.13
80. Clay bowl M 712[4] = pot P.14
81. Clay bowl M 712[4] = pot P.15

82. Clay bowl M 712[4] = pot P.16

83. Clay bowl M 712[4] = pot P.17

84. Hammerstone M 712[39]

85. Saucer/lid M 712[82] = pot P.81

86. Spindle whorl M 712[75]

87. Faience plaque M 712[59]

87a. Clay ring with incised design M 712

10. OBJECTS FROM GARSTANG'S EXCAVATIONS IN MUSEUM COLLECTIONS

Garstang's excavations at Meroe were financially supported by a number of institutions and wealthy individuals. At the end of each field campaign artefacts were divided up and passed on to the benefactors. Although the majority of project supporters came from the United Kingdom, museums and individuals from other countries also contributed. This resulted in a world-wide distribution of finds. Moreover, many private sponsors passed their collections, either through sale or donation, to other countries and museums, especially but not exclusively to the countries of the British Commonwealth. Outside Great Britain museums with substantial holdings from Meroe include renowned institutions such as the Musée d'Art et d'Histoire in Brussels (Werbrouck 1945), Ny Carlsberg Glypthotek in Copenhagen, Musée du Louvre in Paris and the Royal Ontario Museum in Toronto (Grzymski 1987). Many individual objects from these and other collections have been published and the author is presently engaged in the preparation of a catalogue of the Nubian collection in Toronto. Until this and other catalogues are published, even a simple list of museum holdings giving the museum registration number and most basic information is of scholarly value, as exemplified by the publication of the Liverpool Museum collection (Bienkowski and Southworth 1986). It is for this reason that the list of objects from Garstang's excavations at Meroe presently kept in the Sudan National Museum in Khartoum and the Royal Ontario Museum in Toronto is presented below.

OBJECTS IN THE SUDAN NATIONAL MUSEUM

The list of objects presented below is based on the museum registration numbers. Often, especially in case of loose beads, the same register number is given to more than one object. All the registration numbers listed below, except SNM 531, were assigned to the objects from Garstang's excavations at Meroe. In a few instances, it also includes copies made for the Khartoum museum of objects given to other institutions.

509. Stela of Yesbokheamani from M 6 (Garstang 1911:Pl.XXIV; REM 0407)
510. Gold Kheper ornament from M 261
511. Part of a treasure from Royal Palace: 3 inscribed spacers (one being a facsimile), gold nuggets, metal ring, eight gold and bronze discs
512. Green glaze scarab from Royal City
513. One of the two jars which contained the treasure listed as No.511 and 512
514. Moulders' core or matrice from M 260 (Garstang 1911:Pl.X)
515. Moulders' core or matrice
516. Wooden model of temple pylon from M 6; copy, original in Liverpool (Garstang 1911:Pl.XXII,l)
517. Figurine of a king from M 6 (Garstang 1911:Pl.XXII,3)
518. Faience glazed seal (Garstang 1911:Pl.XXII,4, right; Wenig 1978: cat.116)
519. Small lion emblem from M 6 (Garstang 1911:Pl.XXII,2, right)
520. Decorative emblem cast in bronze (Garstang 1911:Pl.XXII,4)

521. Votive tablet of Horus-on-crocodile, inscribed; from M 260 (Garstang 1911:Pl.XI)

522. Black stone stele depicting a ram-headed god and a queen

523. Fragment of a stele from M 6 (Garstang 1911:Pl.XXIII)

524. Fragments of glazed tiles from Keniseh M 600

525. Glass toilet bottle from tomb 300

526. Two specimens of basketry from the Necropolis

527. Two ornamental staff heads from Tomb 3

528. Facsimile of a votive tablet (Garstang 1911:Pl.I)

529. Meroitic tombstone

530. Carved sculpted head

531. Fragments from Wad Ben Naga

532. Inscribed offering table (Garstang 1911:Pl.LVI, No.2)

533. Inscribed offering table (Garstang 1911:Pl.LVI, No.3)

534. Inscribed offering table (Garstang 1911 :Pl.LVI, No.5)

535. Inscribed offering table (Garstang 1911:Pl.LVII, No.3)

536. Inscribed offering table (Garstang 1911:Pl.LV, No.3)

537. Male figure from palace M 295 (Garstang 1913:Pl.IX)

538. Female figure from palace M 295 (Garstang 1912a:Pl.IX)

539. Burnished black vessel

540. Burnished black-brown vessel of same from as No.539, with incised design round the neck

541. Burnished brown-black vessel, same form as No.540

542. Burnished black vessel similar to No.541 with incised design

543. Burnished black vessel similar to No.541; from grave 341

544. Burnished black vessel, same form as No.540

545. Black burnished vessel, same form as No.540; from grave 324

546. Black burnished vessel, same form as No.540

547. Black burnished bowl

548. Black burnished bowl similar to No.547; from grave 329

549. Black burnished bowl

550. Black burnished cup with incised pattern

551. Black burnished cup, similar to No.550

552. Small black burnished cup, similar to No.550

553. Black burnished cup, red brown in parts, similar to No.550

554. Black burnished shallow dish

555. Red burnished dish, same form as No.550; from grave 309

556. Red burnished bowl of form No.547; from grave 324

557. Red burnished bowl of form No.547; from grave 304

558. Red, highly burnished bowl of form No.547; from grave 300

559. Red, highly burnished bowl of form No.547; from grave 309

560. Dark red bowl of form No.549; from grave 304

561. Small red cup with lip

562. Burnished red pottery stand decorated with vertical white bands; from grave 329

563. Burnished red pottery stand decorated with painted white lines

564. Burnished red pottery stand, with painted white decoration

565. Burnished red pottery stand with painted white decoration; from grave 304N

566. Burnished red pottery stand with painted white decoration

567. Large red ware vessel; from grave 307

568. Large red ware vessel of form No.567 with neck decorated with two broad white bands; from grave 307

569. Large red ware vessel of form No.567 with traces of white band decoration; from grave 307

570. Large red ware vessel of form No.567 with red burnished neck and white band decoration; from grave 307

571. Red ware vessel of form No.567; from grave 307

572. Red ware vessel with traces of red burnish and white band decoration

573. Red ware vessel with traces of red burnish and white band decoration

574. Red ware vessel similar to No.573

575. Red ware vessel similar to No.573 with red burnished neck and white band decoration

576. Red ware vessel similar to No.572

577. Red ware vessel

578. Red ware vessel of form No.573 with traces of red burnish and painted white band decoration

579. Red were vessel similar to No.578

580a. Red ware vessel of form No.573; found in Garstang's dig house and brought to the museum in 1929

580. Red ware vessel of form No.573; presented to Mr. Pole 15.12.1923

581. Red ware vessel with red burnished neck and painted broad white band

582. Red ware vessel of form No.577

583. Reddish black vessel of form No.577

584. Red ware vessel of form No.573

585. Undecorated red-yellow ware vessel of shape similar to No.573

586. Red ware vessel of form No.573

587. Red ware vessel of form No.572

588. Red ware vessel of form No.573 with red burnished neck and painted red-white decoration

589. Black vessel of form No.577

590. Red ware vessel

591. Black burnished bowl of form No.553

592. Black burnished bowl of form No.553

593. Black burnished bowl of form No.553

594. Black burnished bowl of form No.553

595. Black burnished bowl of form No.553

596. Black burnished bowl of form No.553

597. Black burnished bowl of form No.553

598. Black burnished bowl of form No.553

599. Black burnished bowl of form No.549

600. Red burnished bowl of form No.553

601. Red ware vessel with a spout

602. Clay spindle whorl

603. Clay spindle whorl painted red and white

604. Red clay spindle whorl

605. Clay spindle whorl

606. Clay spindle whorl

607. Clay spindle whorl

608. Three blue lotus leaf amulets

609. Two buttons, one yellow and one green, from M 294

610. Small blue faience pendant

611. Small open-work faience amulet

612. Bronze signet ring

613. Small garnet(?) seal

614. Small clay seal impression

615. Faience "New Year" ring inscription

616. Faience scarab

617. Two small faience ram heads

618. Bronze finger ring

619. Axe head of diabase

620. Small polished diorite axe head

621. Pendent-shaped banded hornstone

622. Axe head of diabase

623. Head of sistrum with a Hathor head; blue-green faience

623a. Handle of an object in the shape of a sceptre, originally catalogued as belonging with the sistrum

624. Lion-headed female figurine of blue-green faience with two cartouches, one of Aspelta

625. Large open-work barrel-shaped bead

626. Faience fragments of arms with two cartouches of Aspelta

627. Facsimile of faience model of Sun altar(?) approached by steps

628. Bronze jug

629. Bronze situla from tomb 8000

630. Bronze lamp with incised design, large leaf at back and a long handle; presumably from M 294 (see Garstang 1912a:Pl.V.2)

631. Two bronze rings; from the north side of painted wall (M 292? -K.G.)

632. Bronze cow bell

633. Bronze cup with incised design

634. Bronze fragment of a seated figure with a solar disc; from the royal palace

635. Large seal with hieroglyphs; from the royal palace

636. Bronze bowl

637. Bronze bowl

638. Bronze bowl

639. Small bronze bell

640. Three bronze discs

641. Two bronze kohl sticks

642. Bronze Hathor head covered with gold foil

643. Cast of bronze head of Augustus

644. Faience figure of Isis and Horns

645. Eight fragments of coloured glass

646. Sixty-five cubical tesserae

647. Large black heart-shaped pendant

648. Decorated and perforated vessel; restored

649. Goblet decorated with brown line design

650. Bowl with incised design and red and brown decoration

651. Clay vessel with incised design

652. Clay vessel similar to No.651

653. Mud stopper with seal impression

654. Mud stopper with seal impression

655. Mud stopper with seal impression

656. Mud stopper with seal impression

657. Mud stopper with seal impression

658. Mud stopper with seal impression

659. Mud stopper with seal impression

660. Mud stopper with seal impression

661. Mud stopper with seal impression

662. Mud stopper with seal impression

663. Mud stopper with seal impression

664. Faience signet ring

665. Broken figure fragments: head and shoulders

666. Broken faience ram's head

667. Fragment of faience head dress

668. Faience ram's head

669. Seal inscribed on both sides

670. Very small head

671. String of ten beads

672. String of approximately 425 faience beads

673. String of approximately 370 faience beads

674. String of 127 faience beads

675. String of 333 faience beads

676. Long string of approximately 500 faience beads

677. String of 70 faience beads

678. String of 2744 small faience beads

680. String of 138 faience beads

681. Three beads

682. String of 566 faience beads

683. String of 45 garnet beads

684. String of 379 faience beads

685. String of 2563 beads (some presented to the Gold Coast Museum in April 1952)

686. String of 213 faience beads, cowrie shells and garnet beads

687. String of 96 faience beads

688. String of 53 faience amulets

689. String of cowrie shell and 20 faience imitation cowrie shells; also 15 unstrung cowrie shells

690. Large blue faience ram's head

OBJECTS IN THE
ROYAL ONTARIO MUSEUM

The Meroe collection at the Royal Ontario Museum was thought to have come from a bequest of Sir Robert Mond, one of the museum's major benefactors. However, research in the archives of the Royal Ontario Museum and the University of Liverpool showed clearly that it was Sir Edmund Walker, the first chairman of the newly established Toronto museum, who contributed financially to Garstang's excavations and received a selection of finds in return (see Grzymski 1987:15). It is impossible to establish whether the Toronto collection represents exclusively Walker's share or was enhanced by an additional gift from Mond. All the objects were given 921. (=1921) series number, however only 53 of them were originally entered into the system, while the remainder were catalogued in 1977. In 1930 the museum acquired one vessel from the McGregor collection; a polished red bowl 930.14.59. Finally, in 1985 Shinnie transferred to the Royal Ontario Museum all the objects from the Khartoum–Calgary excavations that were assigned to the University of Calgary. These are listed in his publication and do not need to be repeated here. Since the full catalogue of the Royal Ontario Museum Nubian collection is presently being prepared only the basic listing is provided in the present report.

921.4.1. Faience column base from M 200 (Hofmann 1989:108-111)
921.4.2. Pot, stamped decoration
921.4.3. Bowl, stamped decoartion
921.4.4. Pot, heavily reconstructed, stamped decoration
921.4.5. Bowl, painted decoration
921.4.6. Relief fragment with Khonsu
921.4.7. Relief fragment with Isis, M 70 (Török 1997:pl.4)
921.4.8. Offering table, inscribed
921.4.9. Offering table, inscribed
921.4.10. Bowl, red polished with modelled altar design
921.4.11. Bowl, stamped decoration
921.4.12. Cup, heavily reconstructed
921.4.13. cancelled
921.4.14. Cup, heavily restored, marked "900 M B"
921.4.15. Pot, painted vine leaf design, marked "925...K"
921.4.16. Vase, restored, stamped decoration
921.4.17. Sculptured sandstone child head
921.4.18. Faience plaque, M 924 (Garstang and George 1913:6, Pl. IV,4)
921.4.19. Sandstone head, probably from the "Royal Bath" M 195 (Török 1997:pl.48, far right)
921.4.20. Faience plaque with decorative cartouche
921.4.21. Sandstone sculpture of a hedgehog
921.4.22. Faience tile
921.4.23. Faience tile
921.4.24. Bronze figurine of an antelope
921.4.25. Yellow sandstone block with faience inlay
921.4.26. Faince tile
921.4.27. Faience column fragment
921.4.28. Faience plaque, *tyet* amulet
921.4.29. Faience head, probably Bes
921.4.30. Faience plaque, *tyet* amulet
921.4.31. Pot, de-accessioned
921.4.32. Sandstone sculpture of a bull from the "Royal Bath" (Garstang 1911:Pl.8, no.2)
921.4.33. Pot, red
921.4.34. Faience dish
921.4.35. Bronze hasp
921.4.36. Bronze figurine of Harpokrates, perhaps from M 296
921.4.37. Faience bowl or chalice

921.4.38. Bowl, polished black ware
921.4.39. Bowl, polished black ware
921.4.40. Bowl, red coarse ware
921.4.41. Pot, black ware, marked "385 M 12"
921.4.42. Bowl, black ware, marked "384"
921.4.43. Bowl, greyish-black coarse ware
921.4.44. Bowl, coarse red ware, marked "385 M 12"
921.4.45. Pot, black ware, marked "372 M"
921.4.46. Bowl, coarse red ware
921.4.47. Pot, coarse red ware
921.4.48. Bowl, grey-black ware
921.4.49. Pot, greyish-black ware
921.4.50. Bowl, coarse red ware
921.4.51. Jar, dull brown ware
921.4.52. Pot, reddish brown Alwa ware
921.4.53. Pot, de-accessioned in 1966
921.4.54. Bronze figure of Khonsu
921.4.55. Bronze pin
921.4.56. Minature faience cat amulet
921.4.57. Faience statuette of Nefertem (Grzymski 1994)
921.4.58. String of 244 stone and faience beads
921.4.59. Glass ring
921.4.60. Fragment of faience plaque
921.4.61. Fragment of faience plaque
921.4.62. Globular Alwa ware jar
921.4.63. cancelled
921.4.64. cancelled
921.4.65. cancelled
921.4.66. Globular pot, marked "655"
921.4.67. Footed faience dish
921.4.68. Part of faience dish
921.4.69. String of 541 faience beads from box marked "943 M 13"
921.4.70. Bronze statuette with a tall headdress (Osiris?)
921.4.71. Bronze buckle, from box marked "91 M 12"
921.4.72. Glass bead, from box marked "289 M 12"

921.4.73. Bronze handle
921.4.74. Bronze handle
921.4.75. Bronze knob
921.4.76. Fragment of moulded glass bowl
921.4.77. String of 98 faience beads, from box marked "289 M 12"
921.4.78. String of 45 faience beads, from box marked "289 M 12"
921.4.79. String of 81 faience beads, from box marked "289 M 12"
921.4.80. String of 97 faience beads, from box marked "289 M 12"
921.4.81. Faience *wedjat* eye bead, from box marked "289 M 12"
921.4.82. Faience *wedjat* eye bead, from box marked "289 M 12"
921.4.83. Steatite eye-paint holder, from box marked "289 M 12"
921.4.84.A-H. Eight strips of glass, from box marked "289 M 12"
921.4.85. Glass sherd, from box marked "289 M 12"
921.4.86. Carnelian bead, from box marked "289 M 12"
921.4.87. String of 1390 faience beads, from box marked "M 12 289"
921.4.88. Fragment of faience ram's head amulet
921.4.89. Faience bead, from box marked "920 M 13"
921.4.90. Glass cylinder, from box marked "920 M 13"
921.4.91. Bronze nail, from box marked "911 M 13"
921.4.92. Black stone earplug, from box marked "925"
921.4.93. Ostich eggshell bead, from box marked "925"
921.4.94. Strip of bronze, from box marked "925"
921.4.95. Bronze nail, from box marked "925"
921.4.96. Faience beads
921.4.97. Clay ring, from box marked "920 M 13"

921.4.98. Bronze fitting, from box marked "905 M 13"

921.4.99. Faience footed dish

921.4.100. Ivory earplug

921.4.101. Ostrich eggshell bead

921.4.102. Bronze handle, from box marked "91 M 12"

921.4.103. Bronze handle, from box marked "91 M 12"

921.4.104. Bronze pin, from box marked "91 M 12"

921.4.105. Bronze nail, from box marked "91 M 12"

921.4.106. Bronze handle in form of acanthus leaf, from box marked "91 M 12"

921.4.107. Bronze handle in form of acanthus leaf, from box marked "91 M 12"

921.4.108. Bronze corner brace, from box marked "91 M 12"

921.4.109. Three bronze rivets or decorative bosses, from box marked "91 M 12"

921.4.110. Nine bronze rivets, from box marked "91 M 12"

921.4.111. Bronze coupling, from box marked "91 M 12"

921.4.112. Bronze handle, from box marked "91 M 12"

921.4.113. Strip of bronze, from box marked "91 M 12"

921.4.114. Bronze piece in shape of uraeus hood, from box marked "91 M 12"

921.4.115. Oblong bronze fragment, from box marked "91 M 12"

921.4.116. Fragment of iron key, from box marked "91 M 12"

921.4.117. Faience sherd, from box marked "91 M 12"

921.4.118. Ostrich eggshell bead, from box marked "91 M 12"

921.4.119. Faience spheroid bead, from box marked "91 M 12"

921.4.120. Glass bead, from box marked "91 M 12"

921.4.121. Unbaked clay bead, from box marked "91 M 12"

921.4.122. Faience bead, from box marked "91 M 12"

921.4.123. Glass disc bead, from box marked "91 M 12"

921.4.124. Part of faience amulet, from box marked "91 M 12"

921.4.125. Carved bone fragment

921.4.126. Rectangular worked bone fragment

921.4.127. Triangular worked bone fragment

921.4.128. Oblong worked bone fragment

921.4.129. Triangular worked bone fragment

921.4.130. Fragment of worked bone

921.4.131. Fragment of worked bone

921.4.132. Bone splinter

921.4.133. Oblong ivory fragment

921.4.134. Bronze boss fragment, from box marked "91 M 12"

921.4.135. Bronze inlay

921.4.136. Bronze inlay, from box marked "91 M 12"

921.4.137. Seven small bronze rivets, from box marked "91 M 12"

921.4.138. Decorative bronze plate, from box marked "91 M 12"

921.4.139. Section of bronze vessel, from box marked "91 M 12"

921.4.140. Faience lid

921.4.141. Iron key fragment

921.4.142. Rectangular iron plate

921.4.143. Iron ring

921.4.144. Iron nail

921.4.145. Iron nail

921.4.146. Iron nail

921.4.147. Iron hook

921.4.148. Iron piece, has label attached which reads "900"

921.4.149. Iron piece

921.4.150. Iron piece, perhaps part of handle

921.4.151. Metal cone (iron or brass ?)

921.4.152. Painted potsherd

921.4.153. Painted potsherd

921.4.154.A-D. Four glass sherds, from box marked "91 M 12"

921.4.155. Iron blade tip

921.4.156. Glass (?) sherd, from box marked "91 M 12"

921.4.157. Clay ball, perhaps a gaming piece, from box marked "925"

The list of objects from these two collections is just a tip of an iceberg. As Wenig (1999b:69) has pointed out it would be a truly worthwhile task to assemble a complete list of objects from Meroe now dispersed worldwide. Wenig has mentioned artefacts kept in Edinburgh, Paris, Kopenhagen and other places and thanks to the courtesy of Dr. Luc Limme and his colleagues, this author was able to study the Meroe collection in Brussels (registration numbers E.3103-3173, E.3539-3558, E.3623-3729, E.3973, E.3976-3982, E.4720-4779, E. 4961-4968, E. 5116-5180). In Canada, a small collection of Garstang's objects, both original and replicas, was acquired by the Redpath Museum of the McGill University in Montreal and was published by Berg (1990; see also Trigger 1994).

11. ESTIMATING THE POPULATION SIZE OF MEROE

At the Fourth Meroitic Conference held in Berlin in November 1980 this author presented a brief paper on estimating the population size of various Meroitic settlements based on the study of architectural remains (Grzymski 1984). A more detailed paper on the palaeodemography of Meroe was presented at the African Historical Demography Seminar held at the University of Edinburgh in April 1981 and published later that year (Grzymski 1981). This work attracted the attention of several scholars, some of whom have made comments directly relevant to the question of the population size of Meroe (see especially Török 1997b:44-49 and Edwards 1997c). One feels, therefore, justified in revisiting the subject since it is pertinent to our present field work at Meroe and to the issue of historical demography of the Meroitic Kingdom in general. Admittedly much of what can be said about the population size of Meroe and other Meroitic sites is based on rather crude data and remains speculative. Nevertheless, in order to better understand the social and economic life of ancient people we need to know at least approximate population numbers, a sentiment already expressed by Vercoutter (1970:166 n.29; see also Zibelius-Chen 1988:37-40). Despite the fortuitous way the palaeodemographic data are preserved the contribution of archaeology to the study of human life span and mortality seems to be valued and respected by demographers. Lower Nubia is especially important for more comprehensive studies because it has been studied and excavated so thoroughly as few other areas in the world. Much of the information can be extrapolated and applied to the demographic study of other parts of the Middle Nile Valley. Apart from archaeological data we also possess a certain amount of written sources relevant to Meroitic studies and there is also a good possibility for making direct historical analogies. Physical anthropologists conducting palaeodemographic studies tend to rely exclusively on the skeletal remains. However, non-skeletal approaches to estimating ancient population sizes are also worth exploring as has been demonstrated by historians and cultural anthropologists. These approaches are particularly relevant to our attempts, however crude, of estimating the population size of Meroe.

ESTIMATING POPULATION NUMBERS THROUGH ARCHITECTURAL REMAINS

In his 1962 article R. Naroll argued that there is a direct correlation between the floor space of a house, or more specifically a roofed dwelling, and the population size of a given settlement. He concluded that the average ratio of the total floor space to the site population size is 10:1, although it must be noted that his data, drawn from many different cultures, show a substantial variety.

In the case of the Nile Valley we are fortunate to possess census data from Roman Egypt according to which the average family living in a house numbered 3.5 persons (Russell 1958:64). Since the information was gathered for tax purposes one may assume that it underestimates the occupation density which could have been 4 to 5 persons/house. Considering that the average size of a Meroitic house was 29.85 m^2 (see Grzymski 1984:287-288), the space occupied by one individual would amount to 6 m^2 to 8.5 m^2. If we knew the total site area and what proportion of this area was dwelling space then we could calculate approximate population size of a given settlement. Unfortunately, none of the Meroitic sites have been excavated to such a degree as to permit calculation of dwelling space as a percentage of the total site area. In case of Meroe one can estimate city limits as encompassing the entire fenced area shown on the map published by Shinnie and Bradley (1980:fig.5). Using the modern fence as a boundary line is entirely artificial but the enclosed area does in fact encompass the majority of the presently recognizable remains of the ancient city. Thus, the overall area of ancient Meroe might have been approximately 450,000 to 500,000 m^2, while that of Kawa (Macadam 1955:pl.2,3) about 140,000-150,000 m^2. The area contained within the enclosure wall at Faras (Michałowski 1962:Plan I) was approximately 34,000 m^2. Taking into account the fact that large parts of these sites were occupied by religious (temples) and industrial (workshops) structures only about a third of the total site area could have been occupied by roofed dwellings. This must be further reduced by half to subtract open courts and streets in the domestic quarters of the town. Taking these factors into consideration we can use the following formula:

$$P = 1/6 \ (A_t/A_i)$$
where

P - population size
A_t - total size area
A_i - dwelling space required by one individual

Based on the space requirement of 6 m^2 to 8.5 m^2 per person we would arrive at a total population of between 8,800 and 13,800 inhabitants in Meroe. The population of Kawa would number 2,700 to 4,100, while that of Faras would fall between 660 and 940 inhabitants. It is instructive to note that according to the taxpoll of 171-174 AD the town of Aswan (Syene) had 805 taxpayers suggesting a total population of 2,265 people (Russell 1958:78).

The numbers presented above are, of course, merely estimates. It is possible that at any given time only part of a site was occupied or that the house density was higher (or lower) than that accepted for our calculation purposes. Perhaps improvements could be made by studying modern population sizes and house densities in the present-day villages of Deragab and Kijeik. Edwards (1999c:97) has pointed out that aerial photographs of Meroe suggest that these two villages cover at least as much area as the site itself. Although I had no access to modern census data I understand from discussions with local people that Deragab and Kijeik together have probably about 2,000 inhabitants. It has to be noted, however, that modern properties contain large open spaces (*hosh*). This was not the case in Meroitic times as is clear from the findings presented in this publications and from the discoveries of the Khartoum–Calgary team. It is evident that in Meroe, as well as in other Meroitic sites such as Meinarti, the dwellings were densely clustered. Thus, the population size of between 8,800 and 13,800 people is entirely feasible. It should also be taken into account that there was substantial suburban population in places such as Hamadab and Gadu, both being confirmed archaeological sites and in the yet-to-be-located port of Tadu, known from classical accounts (Priese 1984:496). This is in addition to the areas covered by modern villages of Deragab, Kijeik and Begrawiya. The suggested population size of Meroe, a capital city of a large kingdom, compares favourably with that of Aswan, an important but provincial town in contemporary Egypt. These numbers also seem reasonable when compared to the estimated total population of Meroitic Empire discussed below.

ESTIMATING POPULATION SIZE THROUGH SKELETAL REMAINS

The first Nubiologist attempting to estimate the population size of a settlement on the basis of skeletal material was Vila in his study of the Aksha cemetery (Vila 1968:328, 382). The main problem in using skeletal data is the need to know the time interval during which the cemetery was in use, how big a part of the cemetery was excavated, what was the birth rate, female fertility and survivorship as well as the life expectancy. Some of the information may be calculated from the study of human remains in Nubia, in other instances it can be obtained by comparison with the Egyptian data. The classical formula for determining the population size was proposed by Acsadi and Nemeskeri (1970:65-66) and takes into account the number of dead individuals, life expectancy at birth, the period of use of the cemetery and a correction factor. A detailed calculation of the population sizes of Faras (800 to 1,400 people) and Karanog (350 to 600

people) was presented in my 1981 study and need not be repeated here. Perhaps the most remarkable fact was that the calculation of the population size of Faras by means of different techniques, i.e. through the study of the architectural and anthropological remains, produced very similar results. Due to the lack of skeletal material from Meroe this approach is presently not possible in our study of the population size of this particular site.[9] I have also suggested there that the population size of Meroitic Lower Nubia was approximately 10,000. This was substantially less than Trigger's estimated 60,000 inhabitants in all of Lower Nubia, i.e. approximately 40,000 in the Meroitic part of Lower Nubia (Trigger 1965:160). More recently Edwards (1999c:77) proposed an even more dramatic reduction of the population size of Meroitic Lower Nubia to approximately 2,700, a view not shared by this author.

NON-SKELETAL APPROACHES TO ESTIMATING MEROITIC POPULATION SIZE

Among many concepts and ideas developed within the framework of ecological archaeology one that is most relevant for this study is the so-called "Carrying Capacity Concept." The carrying capacity can be somewhat simplistically defined as "the maximum size of population which can be maintained indefinitely within an area" (Zubrow 1975:15). In order to make

---

[9]The absence of the Meroitic period cemeteries near Meroe is difficult to explain. It is unlikely that the only inhabitants of Meroe to be buried near the city were rulers, high officials, and members of the royal family interred in the tombs in the West, South and North Cemeteries.

estimate of the population size on the basis of the carrying capacity of the lands the given population lived on one has to know the following:

(...)(a) what resources are exploited and what are their abundances, (b) how the resources are exploited, (c) the degree of dependence on each resource, and (d) the viability of the resources under different levels of exploitation.

(Glassow 1978:37).

Archaeological discoveries at Meroe, Qasr Ibrim and other sites, as well as the famous petroglyph at Jebel Geili point to grain, and specifically to sorghum, as the main element of the Nubian diet. In the southern part of the Meroitic Kingdom cattle could also have been of some importance. Written documents from Egypt indicate that the ordinary yield of grain was 1600 *ḥḳ3t* per aroura and that an average individual, presumably with his family, cultivated about 10 arouras (Baer 1962, 1963; for Egyptian measures see appendix 11.1). Ecological observations, especially those presented in the well-known publication edited by Tothill (1948) provide an invaluable insight into the methods of agriculture in the areas that once formed the core of the Meroitic Kingdom. Thanks to Tothill's account we can draw a picture of what the land cultivation in the Nile Valley looked like before the introduction of modern technologies in Nubian agriculture. This, of course, has been long recognized by scholars engaged in the study of the economy and ecology of Meroitic Nubia (e.g. Ahmed 1984, 1999a; Edwards 1989, 1995, 1999b; Trigger 1965).

Generally speaking, the areas on which the Meroitic civilization developed contain four types of arable lands: (a) rainfall watered lands, (b) basin lands, (c) seluka lands, and (d) saqia and shaduf lands. Saqia was introduced to Egypt in Ptolemaic times and was almost certainly common by the second half of the 3rd century BC. It is depicted in an Alexandrian tomb painting dated to the 2nd century BC.[10] If we accept the 1st century BC – 1st century AD as the date of wide-spread daily use of saqia in the Sudan, then the calculations based on the amount of saqia land will be valid mainly for the first few centuries AD. According to Tothill, the arable land of the Northern Province (before the recent administrative reforms) in the Sudan covered only 500 square miles. Although the Nile level is assumed to be a little lower than it was during the Meroitic period (Trigger 1965:166) any supposed land loss would be balanced by the pump irrigation of modern times. We can safely assume, then, that the cultivable area remained relatively stable throughout the last two thousand years. According to Baer the density of rural population in ancient Egypt was 0.5 person/aroura (Baer 1962:113). The soil fertility and agricultural technology in the ancient Sudanese Nile Valley were similar to those of Egypt, therefore Baer's formula is applicable to the Sudan. The area of 500 square miles equals 473,492 arouras, which would suggest a rural population of 236,746 people. According to Baer this rural population would have been able to support half its number of people living in towns. Russell (1958:80), however, suggests that this ratio is smaller, namely 1:8. On this basis we

---

[10]For the history of the saqia see Oleson 1984. The detailed analysis of the tomb scene is offered by Venit 1988:fig.4 and pp.86-87.

could calculate a total population of the Kingdom of Meroe at around 270,000:

rural population - 236,746
urban-population - 29,593
population of Egyptian Nubia[11] - 5,000

In another publication Russell (1966:70-71) stated that an average family holding in the Nile Valley was about 10 arouras, with a family unit of five or six persons. This implies the size of the rural population varying between approximately 237,000 and 284,000. In the latter case the total population of the Meroitic Kingdom would amount to almost 325,000 (rural: 284,000; urban: 35,500; Dodecaschoinos: 5,000).

An interesting study by Jenny (1962) based on a calculation of the amount of nitrogen in the Nile soil and the amount of protein that may be provided by this soil suggests a maximum population density of 1.18 person/aroura. This equals 0.6 person/aroura on a half crop basis (half had to be saved for sowing) and translates into 324,607 people as the maximum number of Meroites that could have been supported by the Nile floods.

Another way of estimating the maximum number of people in the Meroitic Kingdom is by calculating the daily amount of calories that is or may be produced on the arable lands. In the interest of simplification sorghum was chosen as a mean of calculating caloric production of Meroe, although onions, dates and meat were clearly also an important part of the diet. One feddan of basin lands normally gives 300 kg yields of sorghum (Tothill 1948:744). With seluka land giving higher yields, and rain-grown cultivation lower ones, we can accept 300 kg as an overall average for the whole arable land in Meroe. Assuming that the caloric value of modern sorghum is 354 calories/100 gram (Burgess and Burgess 1972:55), that each individual takes 2500 calories daily and that 1/2 of a total crop is consumed by people, then the size of the Meroitic rural population would be 179,384 and with 1/8 of this number basing their subsistence on non-agricultural activities (plus 5,000 inhabitants of the Egyptian Meroitic Nubia) we would end up with almost 230,000 people living in the Meroitic Kingdom.

The calculations presented above are based entirely on the study of the agricultural potential of the areas occupied by the Meroites. No provisions were made for the existence of substantial pastoral population occupying the areas of present-day Keraba and Butana. The field research conducted by Ahmed (1984) and Bradley (1992) was predominantly concerned with the mode of subsistence and means of identifying this transhumant population in the archaeological record rather than attempting to establish the population size (see also Edwards 1999b), although Bradley (1992:40) gives interesting data regarding the size of five modern nomadic households in Northern Kordofan. Ahmed (1999a:297) points out that apart from the sedentary agriculturalists and nomadic pastoralists there were two other groups living in the Island of Meroe: mobile cultivators and hunters.

---

[11]This is the estimated population size of that part of Meroitic Nubia located between Maharaqa and the present-day border between Egypt and Sudan and therefore not discussed by Tothill.

Although the numbers presented here (ranging from 230,000 to 320,000) may seem unimpressive it is worth noticing that the ratio of the relative population sizes of Meroe and ancient Egypt is higher than is the present ratio between the former Northern Province and Egypt. This may explain the relative strength of the Meroitic Kingdom vis-a-vis Egypt. Moreover, since the Meroitic Empire encompassed an area larger than the old Northern Province and also included an indeterminable number of pastoralists the total population size might have approached 300,000 to 400,000 people or perhaps even half a million, as suggested by Hinkel (1997:393). Even this high number is substantially less than Pliny's 250,000 armed men in the Island of Meroe alone (Eide et. al. 1998:886) which would imply a population of about one million.

Appendix 11.1

As the values given to some of the Egyptian units of measurements differ slightly from publication to publication I found it necessary to give here values of the measures of surface and capacity as used in this chapter.

1 aroura = 2735 m^2 = 0.651 feddan = 0.676 acre

1 feddan = 4200 m^2 = 1.536 aroura = 1.038 acre

1 *ḥḳ3t* = 0.135 bushel

BIBLIOGRAPHY

Abbreviations

BzS - Beiträge zur Sudanforschung
CdE - Chronique d'Égypte
GM - Göttinger Miszellen
JAOS - Journal of the American Oriental Society
JARCE - Journal of the American Research Center in Egypt
JSSEA - Journal of the Society for the Study of Egyptian Antiquities
LAAA - Annal of Anthropology and Archaeology. University of Liverpool
MittSAG - Mitteilungen der Sudanarchäologischen Gesellschaft zu Berlin
RCK - The Royal Cemeteries of Kush

Bibliographical List

Acsádi, G. and J. Nemeskéri,
1970, *History of Human Life Span and Mortality*, Budapest

Ahmed, K.A.
1984, *Meroitic Settlement in the Central Sudan*, Oxford
1999a, Economy and Environment in the Empire of Kush, in: Wenig, S., ed. *Studien zum Antiken Sudan* (= *Meroitica* 15): 291-311, Wiesbaden
1999b, The island of Meroe?, in: Wenig S., ed. *Studien zum Antiken Sudan* (= *Meroitica* 15): 457-458, Wiesbaden

Anderson, J. and K. Grzymski
2001, Sudan: Land of the Hidden Temples, *Rotunda* 34 (1): 22-29

Arnold, D.
1999, *Temples of the Last Pharaohs*, New York and Oxford

Baer, K.,
1962, The Low Cost of Land in Ancient Egypt, *JARCE* I: 25-46
1963, An Eleventh Dynasty Farmer's Letters to his Family, *JAOS* 83: 1-19

Berg, D.
1990, The Archaeological Context of the Egyptian and Nubian Antiquities in the Redpath Museum, *Fontanus* 3: 117-130

Bienkowski, P. and E. Southworth
1986, *Egyptian Antiquities in the Liverpool Museum. I. A List of Provenanced Objects*, Warminster

Bradley, R.J.
1982, Varia from the City of Meroe, in: Millet, N.B. and A.L. Kelley, eds., *Meroitic Studies (= Meroitica* 6): 163-170, Berlin
1984a, Meroitic Chronology, in: Hintze, F., ed. *Meroitistische Forschungen 1980 (= Meroitica* 7): 195-211, Berlin
1984b, Wall Paintings from Meroe Townsite, in: Hintze, F., ed., *Meroitistische Forschungen 1980 (= Meroitica* 7): 421-423, Berlin
1992, *Nomads in the Archaeological Record (= Meroitica 13)*, Berlin

Burgess, H.J.L. and A.P. Burgess
1972, Nutritional content and value of local foodstuffs, in: Amann, V.F., D.G.R. Belshaw and J.P. Stanfield, eds., *Nutrition and Food in an African Economy*: 45-58, Kampala

Dunham, D.
1957, *Royal Tombs at Meroe and Barkal*, (=RCK IV), Boston
1963, *The West and South Cemeteries at Meroe*, (=RCK V), Boston

Edwards, D.N.
1989, *Archaeology and Settlement in Upper Nubia in the 1st Millennium AD*, Oxford
1996, *The Archaeology of the Meroitic State. New perspectives on its social and political organisation*, Oxford
1998, Report on The Musawwarat Pottery, *MittSAG* 8: 62-67
1999a, Review of László Török, *Meroe City. An Ancient African Capital*, London 1997, *CdE* LXXIV, 1999: 95-100
1999b, Meroe in the Savannah - Meroe as a Sudanic Kingdom, in: Wenig, S., ed., *Studien zum Antiken Sudan (= Meroitica* 15): 312-320, Wiesbaden
1999c, Meroitic Settlement Archaeology, in: Welsby, D.A., ed., *Recent Research in Kushite History and Archaeology. Proceedings of the 8th International Conference for Meroitic Studies*, London
1999d, *A Meroitic Pottery Workshop at Musawwarat es Sufra (= Meroitica* 17,2), Wiesbaden

Eide, T., T. Hägg, R.H. Pierce and L. Török
1998, *Fontes Historiae Nubiorum*, vol. III, Bergen

Eigner, D.
1996, Die Grabung am Schlackenhügel NW 1 in Meroe, *MittSAG* 4: 23-27
2000, Meroe Joint Excavations: Excavation at Slag Heap NW1 in Meroe, *MittSAG* 10: 74-76

Ernst, H.
1999, Altar oder Thron? Ein Monument Pianchis im Tempel des Amun von Napata, *GM* 173: 73-78

Garstang, J.
1910, Preliminary Note on an Expedition to Meroe in Ethiopia, *LAAA* 3: 57-70

1911, *Excavations at Meroe, Sudan. Second Season, 1910. Guide to the Ninth Annual Exhibition of Antiquities Discovered*, London
1912a, Second Interim Report on the Excavations at Meroe in Ethiopia, *LAAA* 4: 45-52
1912b, *Excavations at Meroe, Sudan, 1912. Guide to the Eleventh Annual Exhibition of Antiquities Discovered*, London
1913, Third Interim Report on the Excavations at Meroe in Ethiopia, *LAAA* 5: 73-83
1914, Fourth Interim Report on the Excavations at Meroe in Ethiopia, *LAAA* 6: 1-21
1914-1916, Fifth Interim Report on the Excavations at Meroe in Ethiopia, *LAAA* 7: 1-24

Garstang, J. and W.S. George
1913, *Excavations at Meroe, Sudan, 1913. Fourth Season. Guide to the Twelfth Annual Exhibition of Antiquities Discovered*, London

Garstang, J. and W.J. Phythian-Adams
1914, *Excavations at Meroe, Sudan, 1914. Fifth Season. Guide to the Thirteenth Annual Exhibition of Antiquities Discovered*, London

Garstang, J., A.J. Sayce and F.Ll. Griffith
1911, *Meroe - City of the Ethiopians*, Oxford

Glassow, M.A.
1978, The Concept of Carrying Capacity in the Study of Culture Process, in: Schiffer, M.B., ed., *Advances in Archaeological Method and Theory*, vol.1: 31-48, New York - San Francisco - London

Grzymski, K.
1981, The Population Size of the Meroitic Kingdom: an Estimation, in: Fyfe. C. and D. McMaster, eds., *African Historical Demography*, vol. II: 259-273, Edinburgh
1984, Population Estimates from Meroitic Architecture, in: Hintze F., ed., *Meroitistische Forschungen 1980* (= *Meroitica* 7): 287-289, Berlin
1987, The Nubian Collection in the Royal Ontario Museum: A Survey, *JSSEA* XVII (1/2): 15-17
1994, A Statuette of Nefertem on a Lion, in: Berger, C., G. Clerc and N. Grimal, eds., *Hommages à Jean Leclant*, vol. 2: 199-202, Le Caire

Hakem, A.M.A.
1988, *Meroitic Architecture. A Background of An African Civilization*, Khartoum

Hinkel, F.
1989, Säule und Interkolumnium in der meroitischen Architektur. Metrologische Vorstudien zu einer Klassifikation der Bauwerke, in: Donadoni, S. and S. Wenig, eds., *Studia Meroitica 1984* (= *Meroitica* 10): 231-267, Berlin
1996, Meroïtische Architektur, in: Wildung, D., ed. *Sudan. Antike Königreiche am Nil*: 391-415, Tübingen

Hintze, F.
1971, *Musawwarat Es Sufra. I.2. Der Löwentempel. Tafelband*, Berlin

Hofmann, I.
1989, Die glasierten Säulenfragmente von M 200 (Meroe - Stadt), Beiträge zur Sudanforschung 4: 107-132

Hofmann, I. and H. Tomandl
1986, Die Widderplastiken in der meroitischen Kunst, *BzS* 1: 58-78

Jenny, H.
1962, Model of Rising Nitrogen Profile in Nile Valley Alluvium and Its Agronomic and Pedogenic Implications, *Soil Society of America. Proceedings* 26 (6): 588-591

Kirwan, L.P.
1960, The Decline and Fall of Meroe, *Kush* 9:163-173

Kormysheva, E.
1994, Das Inthronisationsritual des Königs von Meroe, in: Gundlach, R. and M. Rochgolz, eds., *Ägyptische Tempel - Struktur, Funktion und Programm (= Hildesheimer Ägyptologische Beiträge* 37): 187-210, Hildesheim

Lepsius, C.R.
1849, *Denkmaeler aus Aegypten und Aethiopien*, vol.1

Macadam, M.F.L.
1955, *The Temples of Kawa. II. History and Archaeology of the Site*, London

Michałowski, K.
1962, *Faras. Fouilles Polonaises*, Warszawa

Naroll, R.
1962, Floor Area and Settlement Population, *American Antiquity* 27: 587-589

Oleson, J.P.
1984, *Greek and Roman Mechanical Water-Lifting Devices: the History of a Technology*, Toronto

Priese, K.-H.
1984, Orte des mittleren Niltals in der Überlieferung bis zum Ende des christlichen Mittelalters, in: Hintze, F., ed., *Meroitistische Forschungen 1980 (= Meroitica 7)*: 484-497, Berlin

Robertson, J.H.
1992, History and Archaeology at Meroe, in: Sterner, J. and N. David, eds., *An African Commitment: Papers in honour of Peter Lewis Shinnie*: 35-50, Calgary

Rose, P. and L. Smith
1998, The Pottery, in: Edwards, D., *Gabati. A Meroitic, post-Meroitic and medieval cemetery in central Sudan*: 138-193, London

Russell, J.C.
1958, Late Ancient and Medieval Population, *Transactions of the American Philosophical Society* vol. 48, Philadelphia
1966, The Population of Medieval Egypt, *JARCE* V: 69-82

Sayce, A.H. and J. Gartsang
1910, *Excavations at Meroe, Sudan, 1910. Guide to the Ninth Annual Exhibition of Antiquities Discovered*, London

Seiler, A.
1998, Feine meroitische Ware in Musawwarat es Sufra, *MittSAG* 8: 56-61
1999, Die Keramik - Form und Funktion, in: Fitzenreiter, M., A. Seiler and I. Gerullat, *Die Kleine Anlage (= Meroitica 17,1)*: 53-78, Wiesbaden

Shinnie, P.L.
1974, Meroe in the Sudan, in: Willey, G.R., ed., *Archaeological Researches in Retrospect*: 237-265, Cambridge, Mass.
1984, Excavations at Meroe 1974-1976, in: Hintze, F., ed., *Meroitistische Froschungen 1980 (= Meroitica 7)*: 498-504, Berlin
1987, Meroe 1984/1985, *Nyame Akuma* 28: 48-49

Shinnie, P.L. and J.R. Anderson
in press, *The Capital of Kush 2*, Berlin

Shinnie, P.L. and R.J. Bradley
1980, *The Capital of Kush 1 (= Meroitica 4)*, Berlin

Shinnie, P.L. and F.J. Kense
1982, Meroitic iron working, in: Millet, N.B. and A.L. Kelley, eds. *Meroitic Studies (= Meroitica 6)*: 17-28, Berlin

Tothill, J.D., ed.
1948, *Agriculture in the Sudan*, London

Török, L.
1997a, *Meroe City. An Ancient African Capital*, London
1997b, *The Kingdom of Kush. Handbook of the Napatan-Meroitic Civilization*, Leiden

Trigger, B.G.
1965, *History and Settlement in Lower Nubia*, New Haven

1994, The John Garstang Cylinders from Meroe in the Redpath Museum at McGill University, in: Berger, C., G. Clerc and N. Grimal, eds., *Hommages à Jean Leclant*, vol. 2: 389-398, Le Caire

Tylecote, R.F.
1982, Metal working at Meroe, Sudan, in: Millet, N.B and A.L. Kelley, eds., *Meroitic Studies (= Meroitica* 6): 43-49, Berlin

Venit, M.S.
1988, The Painted Tomb from Wardian and the Decoration of Alexandrian Tombs, *JARCE* XXV: 71-91

Vercoutter, J.
1970, *Mirgissa I*, Paris

Vila, A.
1967, *Aksha II. Le Cimetière Meroïtique d'Aksha*, Paris

Wenig, S.
1994, Meroe Joint Excavations - Bericht über die Vorkampagne 1992, *MittSAG* 1: 15-18
1999a, *Studien zum antiken Sudan. Akten der 7. Internationalen Tagung für meroitistische Forschungen vom 14. bis 19. September 1992 in Gosen/bei Berlin (= Meroitica* 15), Wiesbaden
1999b Review of László Török, *Meroe City. An Ancient African Capital,* London 1997, *MittSAG* 9: 63-69

Werbrouck, M.
1945, Archéologie de Nubie, *Bulletin des musées royaux d'art et d'histoire* 17: 2-9, Bruxelles

Wolf, P.
1996, Vorbericht über die Ausgrabungen am Temple MJE 105, *MittSAG* 4: 28-43

Zibelius-Chen, K.
1988, *Die ägyptische Expansion nach Nubien: Eine Darlegung der Grundfaktoren*, Wiesbaden

Zubrow, E.B.W.
1975, *Prehistoric Carrying Capacity: a Model*, Menlo Park

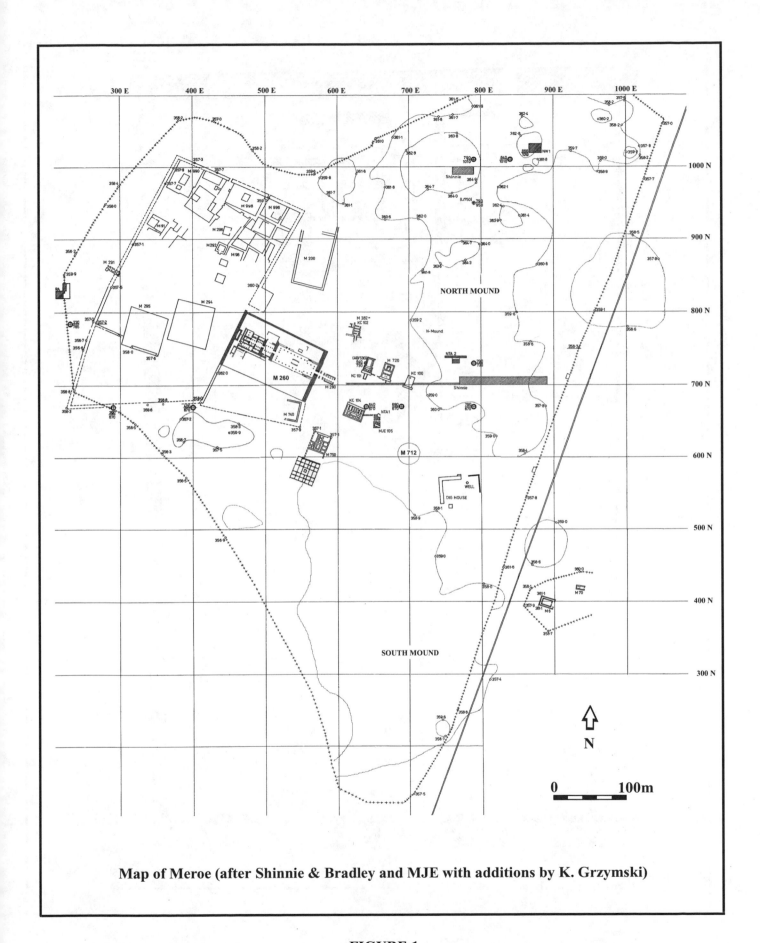

Map of Meroe (after Shinnie & Bradley and MJE with additions by K. Grzymski)

FIGURE 1

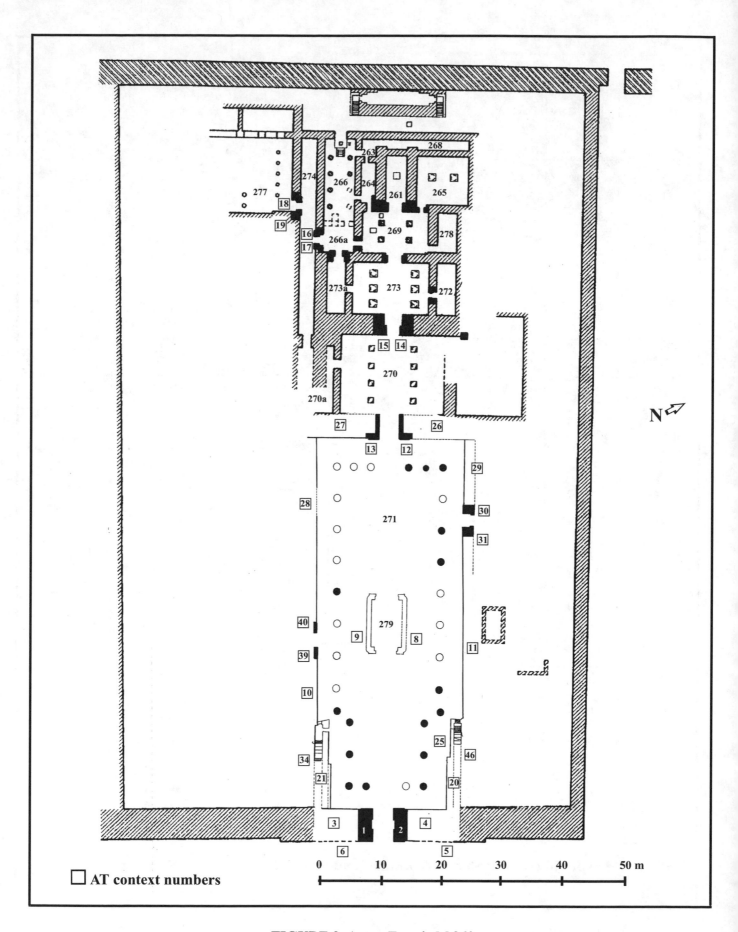

FIGURE 2. Amun Temple M 260

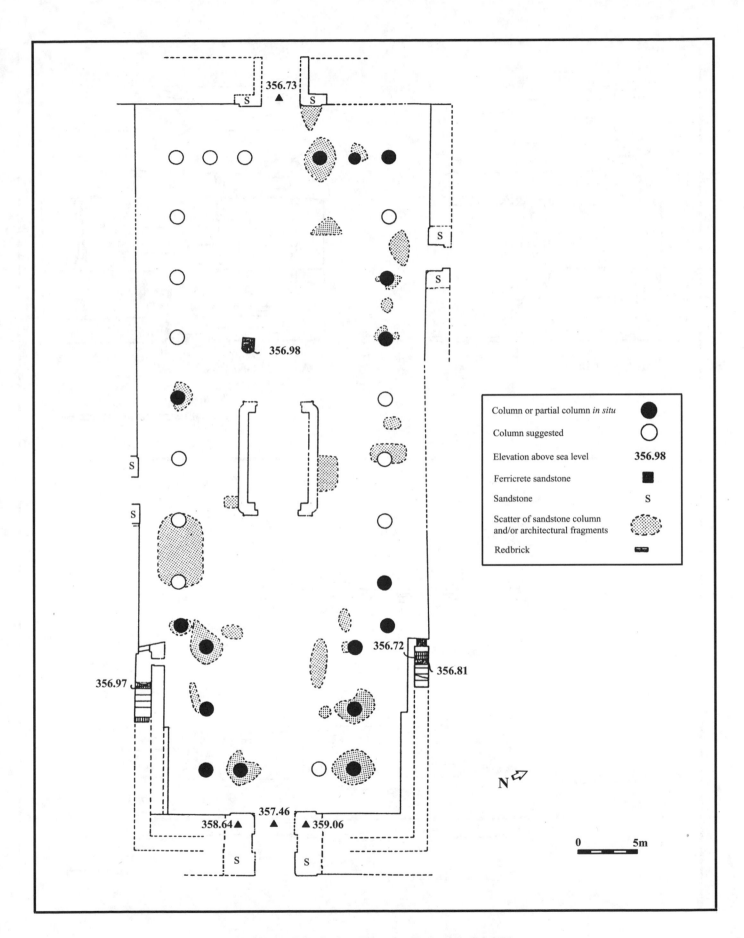

FIGURE 3. Amun Temple, Forecourt M 271

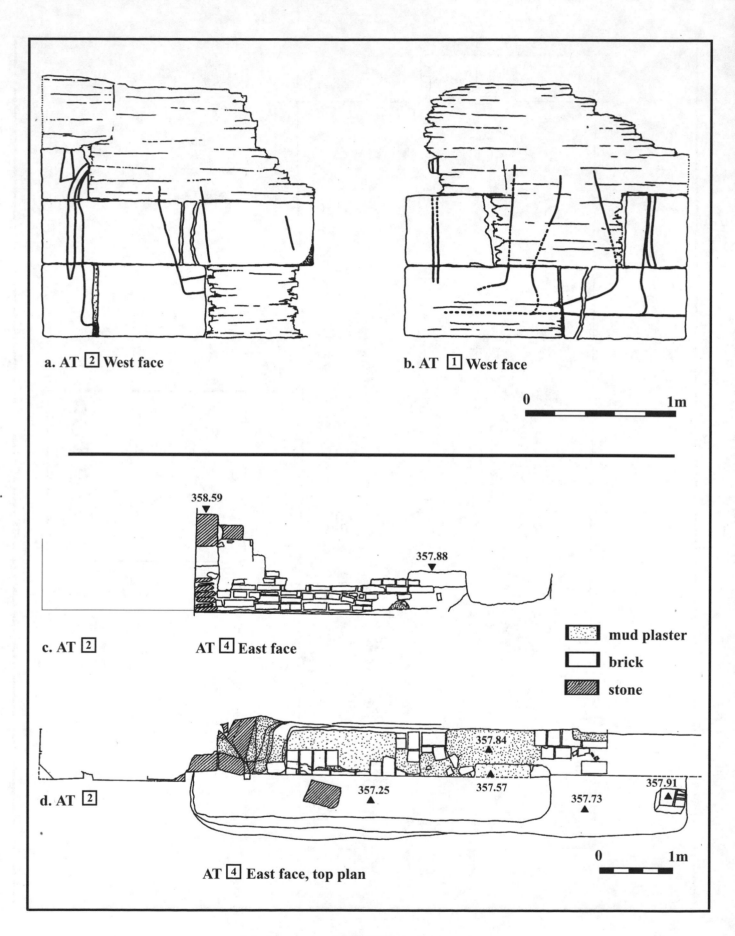

a. AT ② West face

b. AT ① West face

0   1m

358.59

357.88

c. AT ②   AT ④ East face

mud plaster

brick

stone

d. AT ②

357.84

357.25

357.57

357.91

357.73

AT ④ East face, top plan

0   1m

FIGURE 4

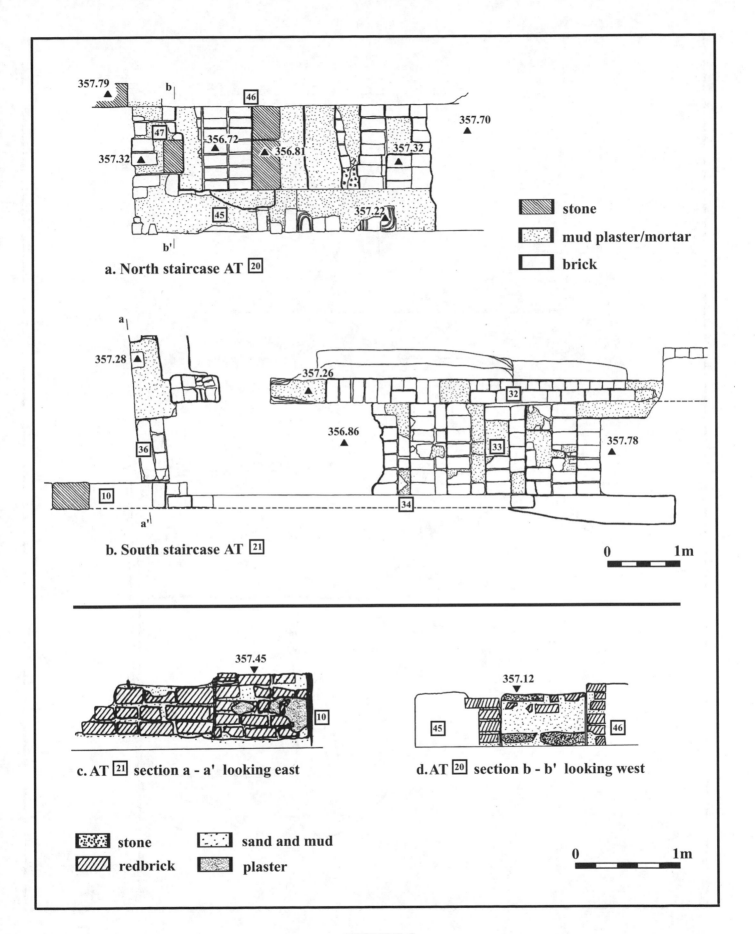

357.79

b

46

47

356.72

357.32

356.81

357.70

357.32

stone

mud plaster/mortar

brick

45

357.22

b'

a. North staircase AT 20

a

357.28

357.26

36

32

356.86

33

357.78

10

34

a'

b. South staircase AT 21

0   1m

357.45

10

357.12

45

46

c. AT 21 **section a - a' looking east**

d. AT 20 **section b - b' looking west**

stone

sand and mud

redbrick

plaster

0   1m

FIGURE 5

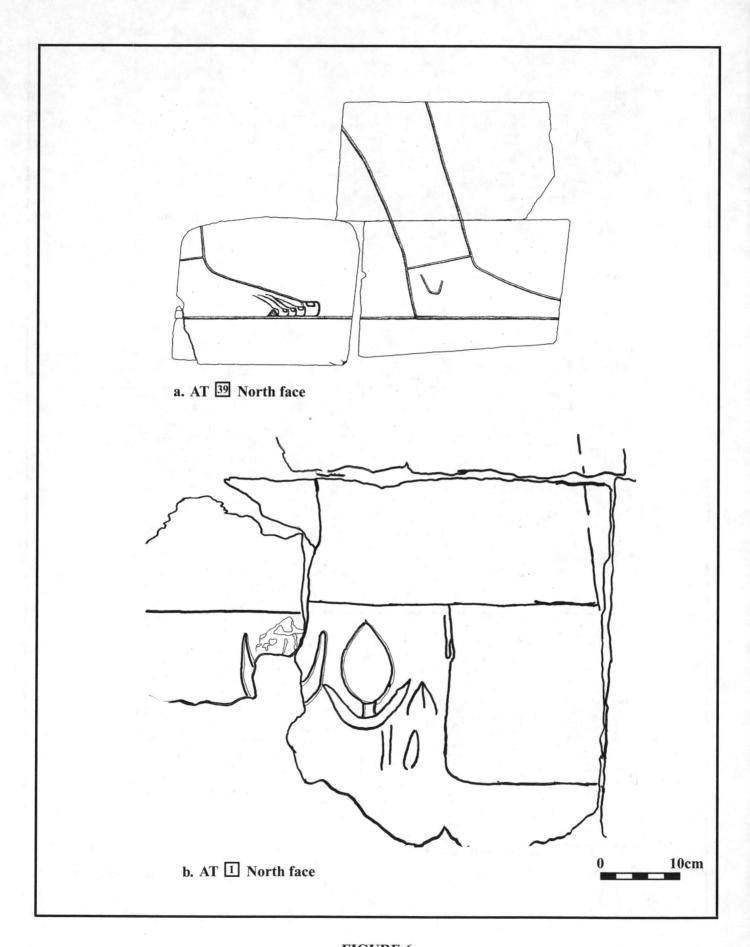

a. AT 39 North face

b. AT 1 North face

0   10cm

FIGURE 6

a. M 271, relief fragment

b. M 271, relief fragment

0   10cm

FIGURE 7

AT ☐17 **South face, graffiti**

0   10cm

FIGURE 8

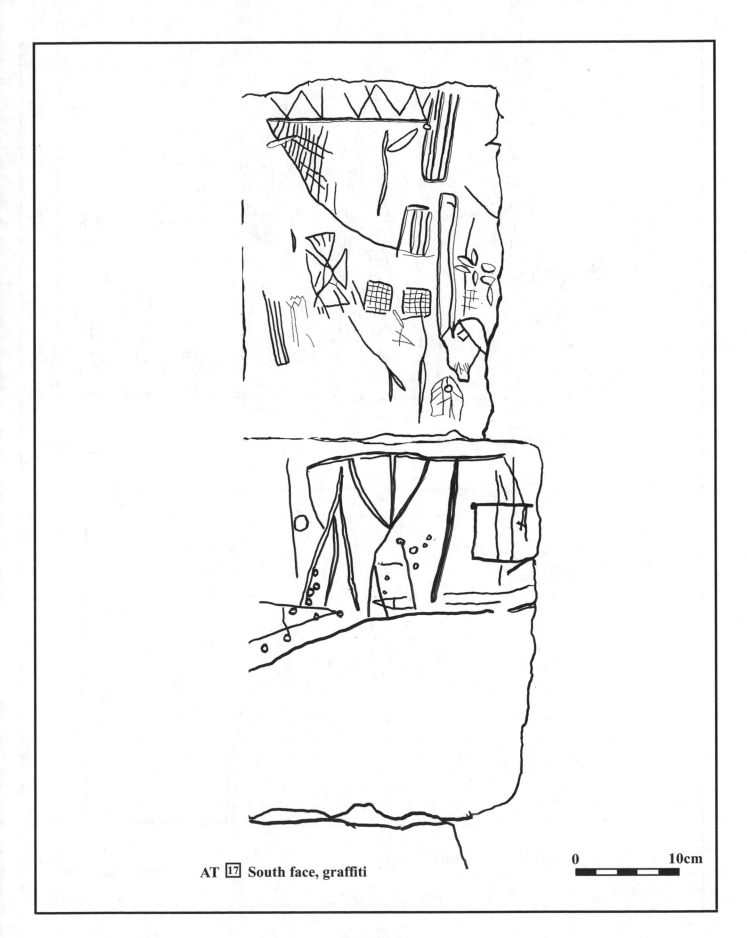

AT 17 South face, graffiti

0   10cm

FIGURE 9

a. AT 16 South face, graffiti

0   10cm

b. AT 16 South face, graffiti

0   10cm

FIGURE 10

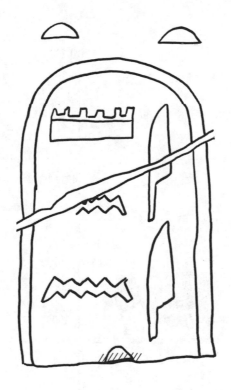

a. Cartouche of Anlamani

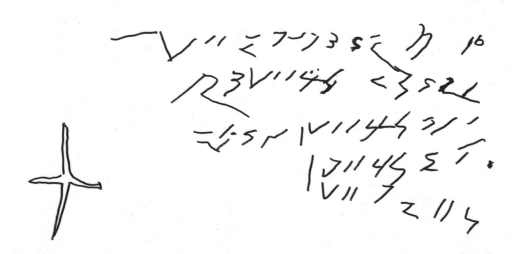

b. AT 16 East face, Meroitic inscription

0   10cm

FIGURE 11

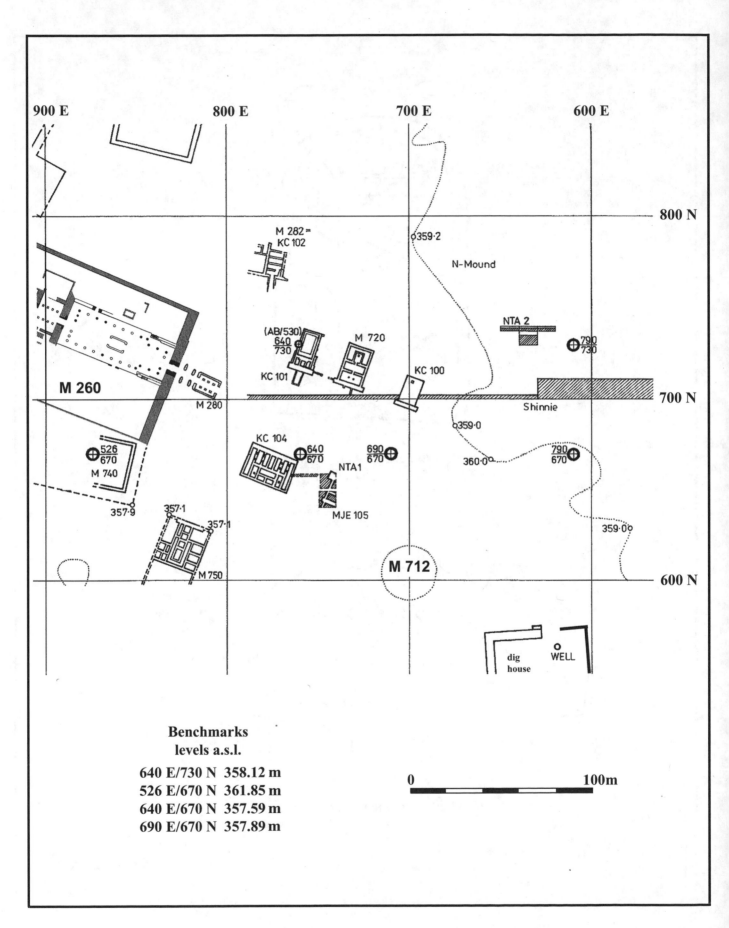

FIGURE 12. Meroe, Processional Way and Mound M 712

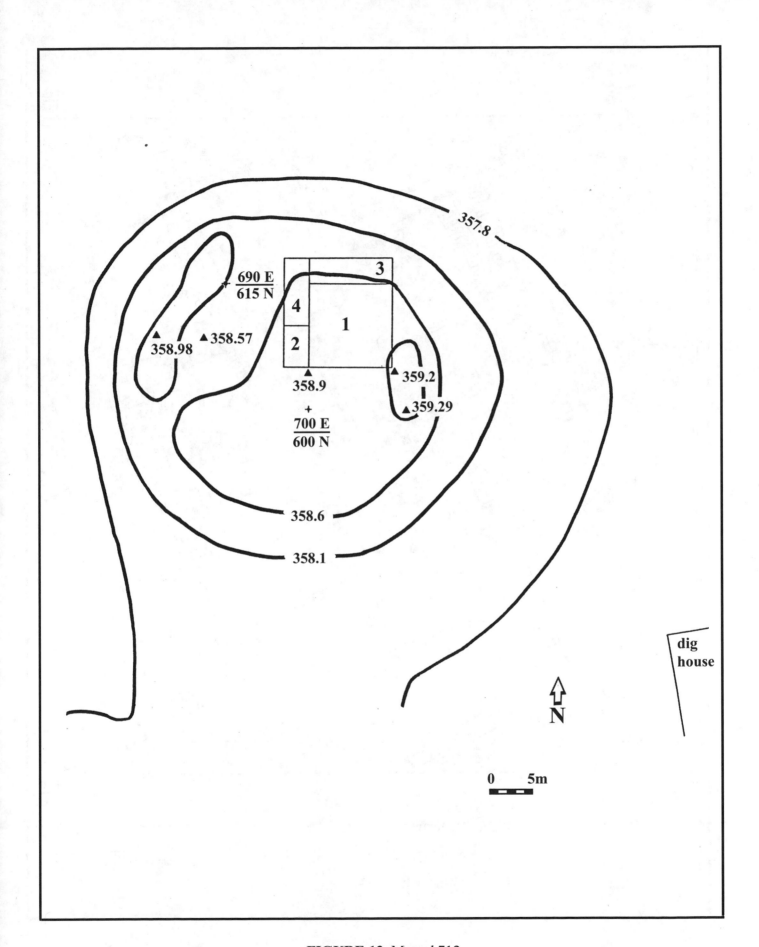

FIGURE 13. Mound 712

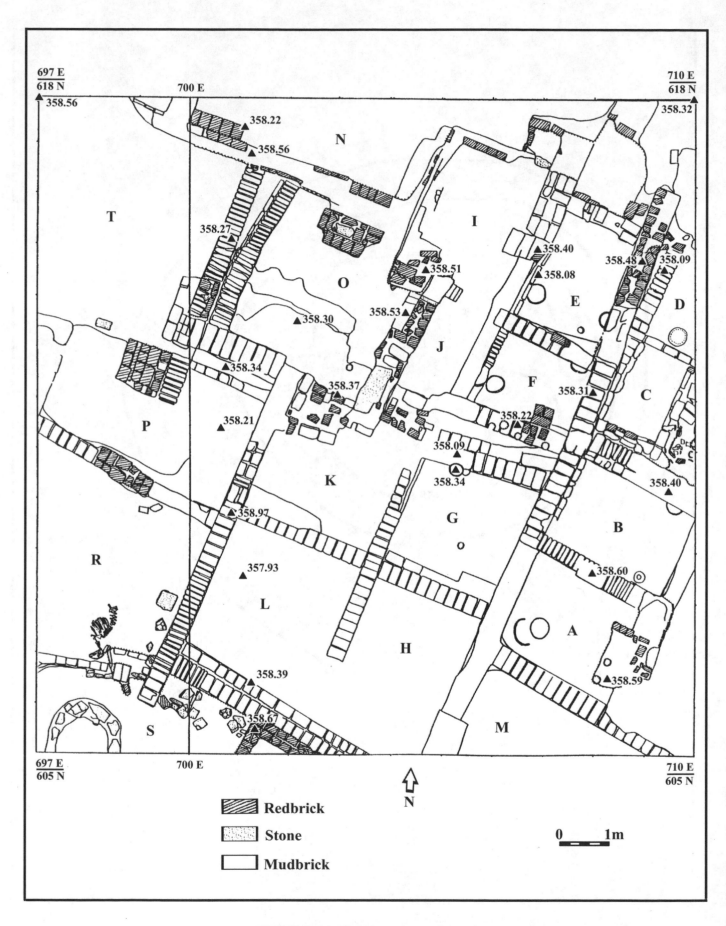

FIGURE 14. M 712, excavated area

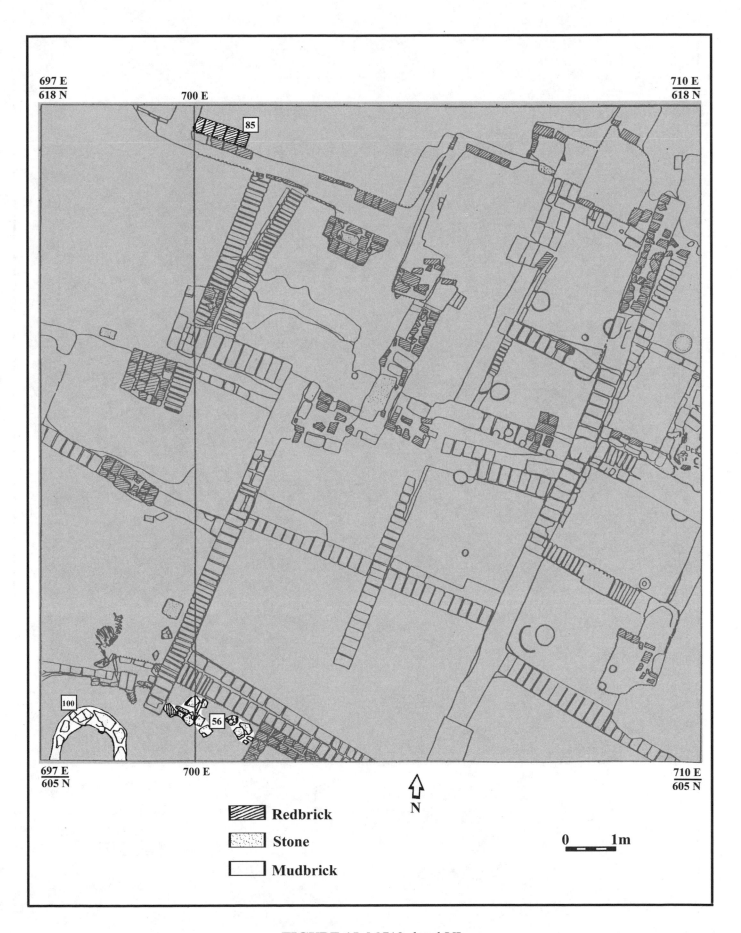

FIGURE 15. M 712, level VI

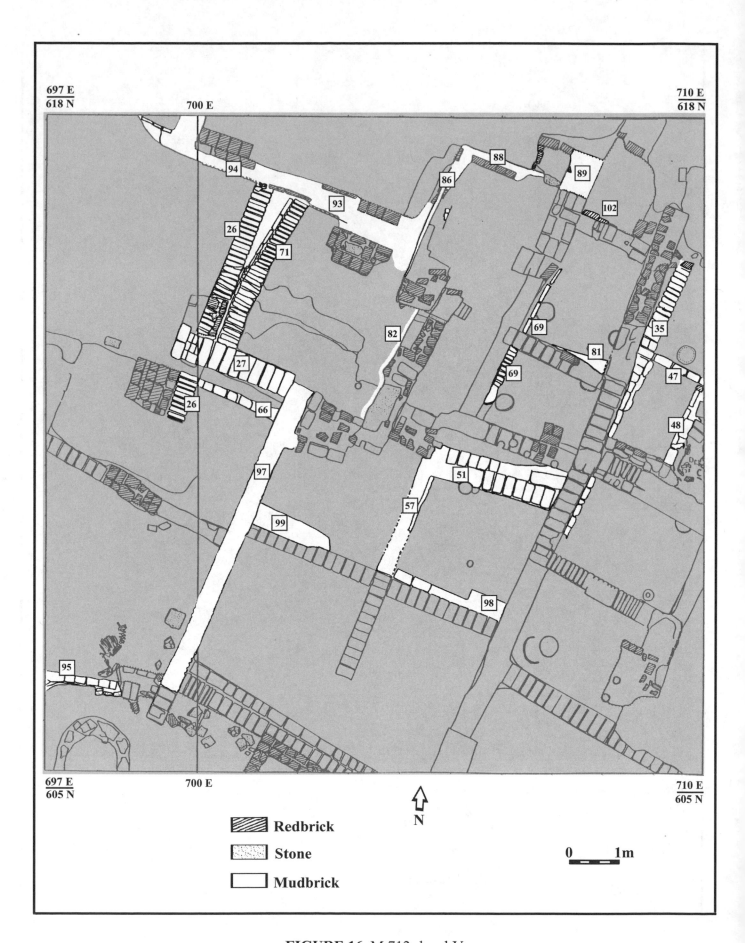

FIGURE 16. M 712, level V

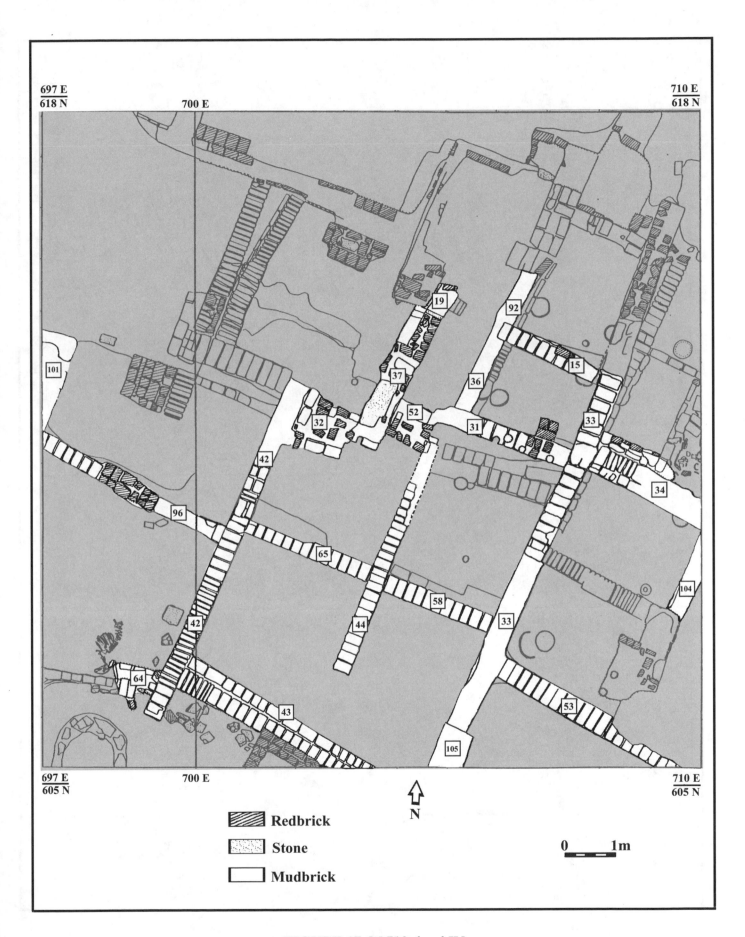

700 E

19

92

101

37

15

36

52

32

31

33

42

96

34

65

42

58

104

44

33

64

53

43

105

700 E

↑
N

Redbrick

Stone

Mudbrick

0   1m

FIGURE 17. M 712, level IV

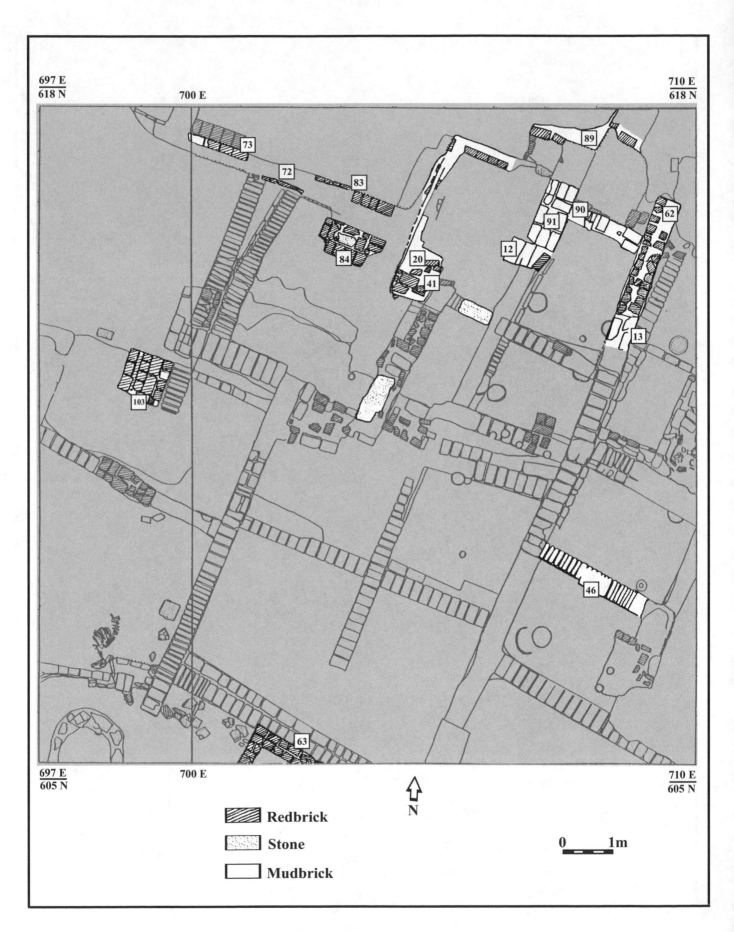

FIGURE 18. M 712, level III

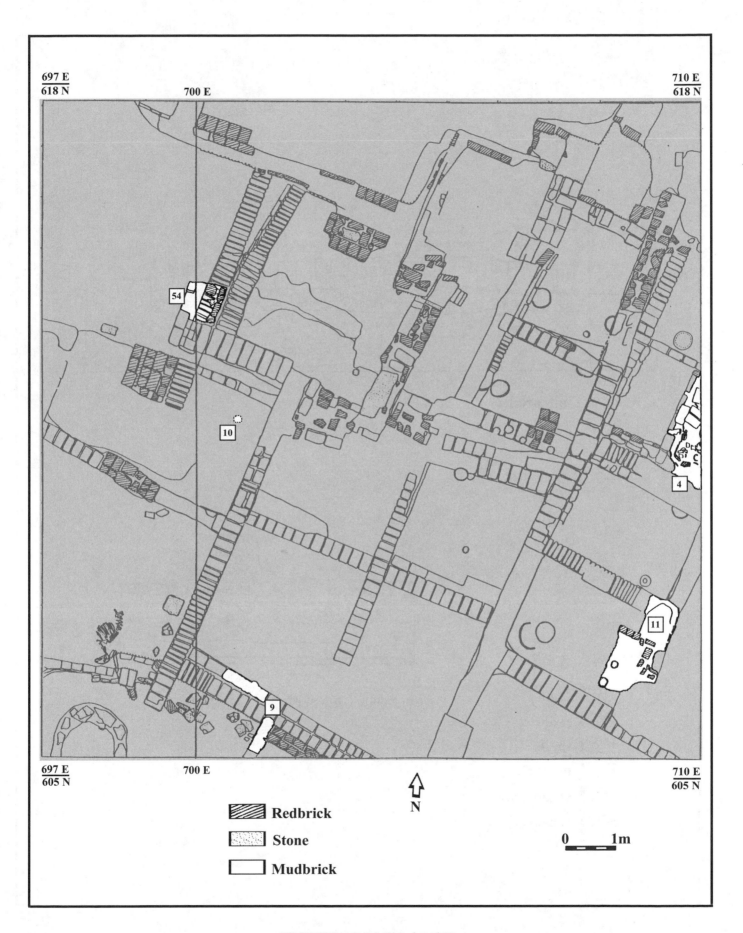

697 E / 618 N 700 E 710 E / 618 N

54

10

4

11

9

697 E / 605 N 700 E 710 E / 605 N

N

Redbrick

Stone

Mudbrick

0   1m

FIGURE 19. M 712, level II

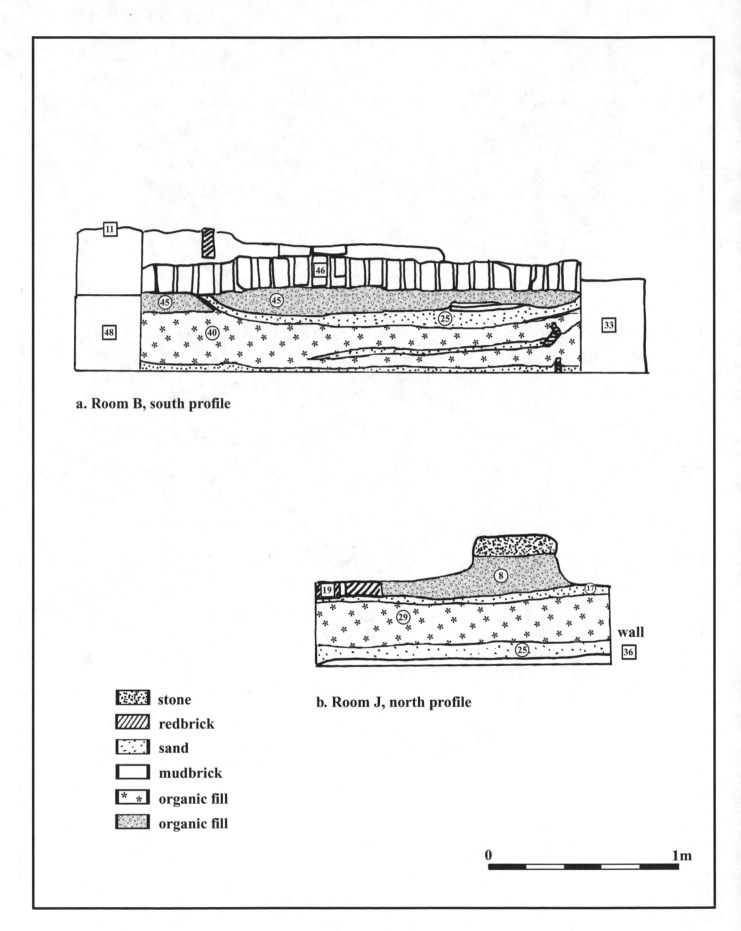

a. Room B, south profile

b. Room J, north profile

wall

stone
redbrick
sand
mudbrick
organic fill
organic fill

0   1m

FIGURE 20. M 712 sections

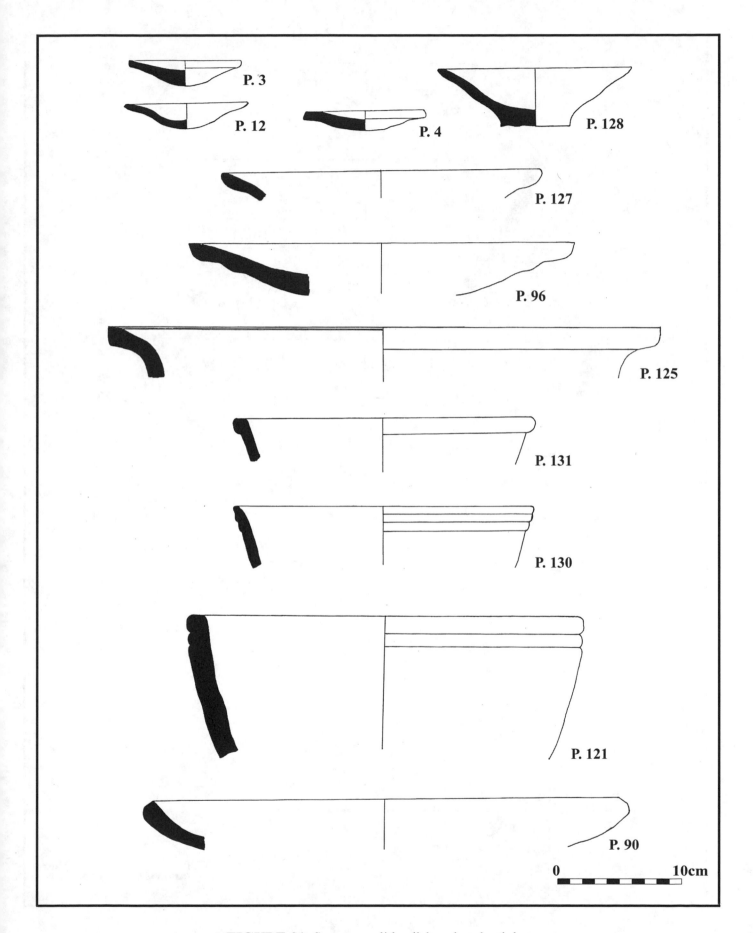

FIGURE 21. Saucers or lids, dishes, bowls, doka

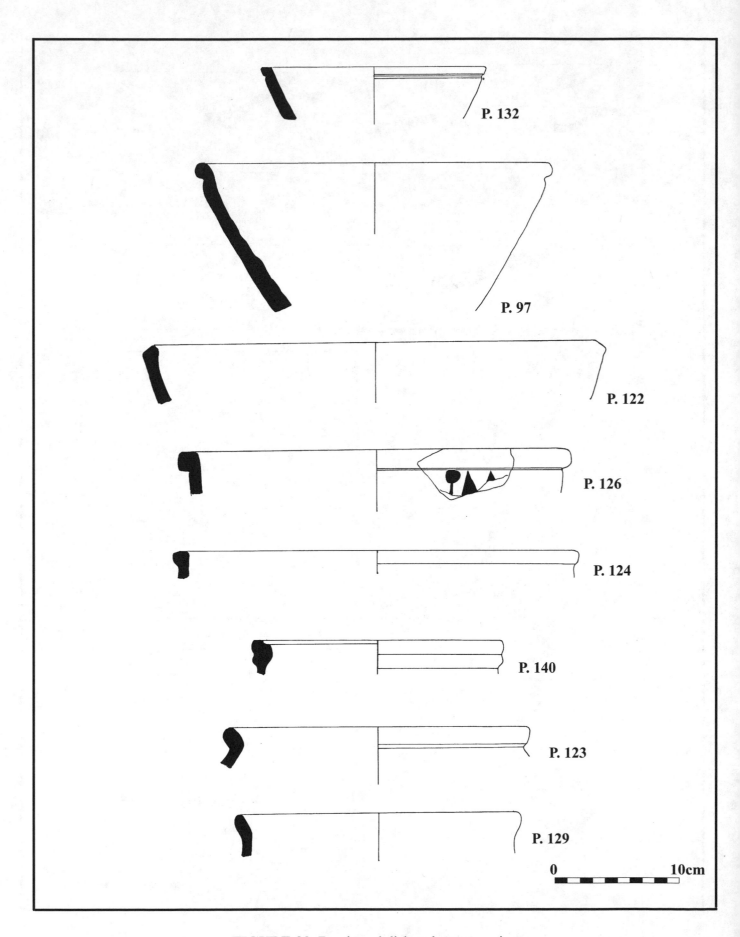

FIGURE 22. Bowls and dishes, large open jars

P. 132

P. 97

P. 122

P. 126

P. 124

P. 140

P. 123

P. 129

0   10cm

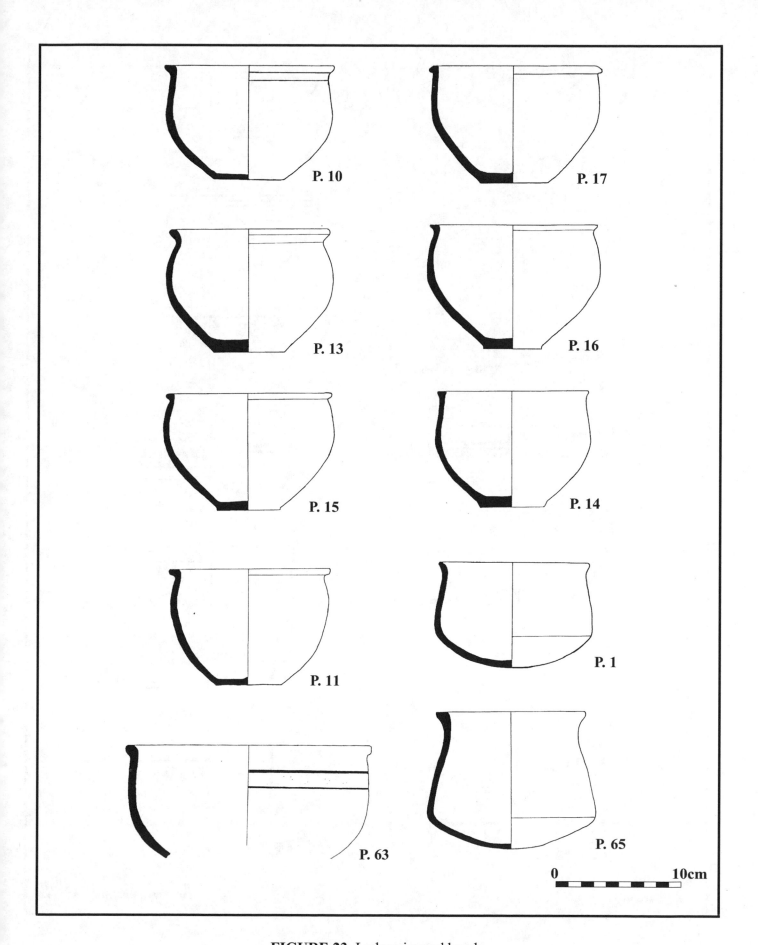

FIGURE 23. Ledge-rimmed bowls

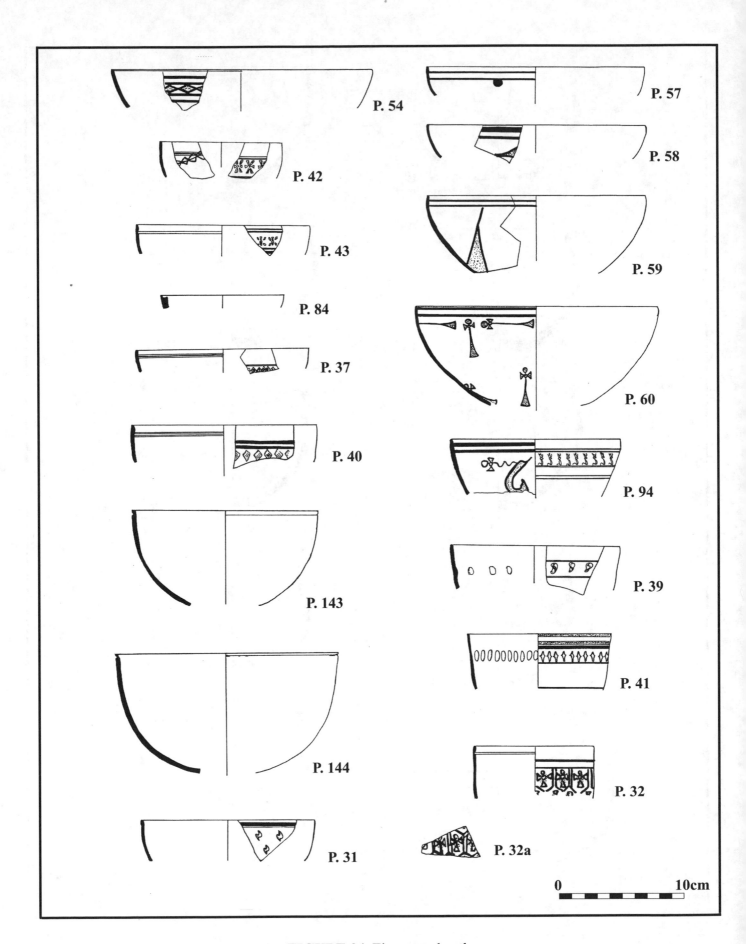

FIGURE 24. Fine ware bowls

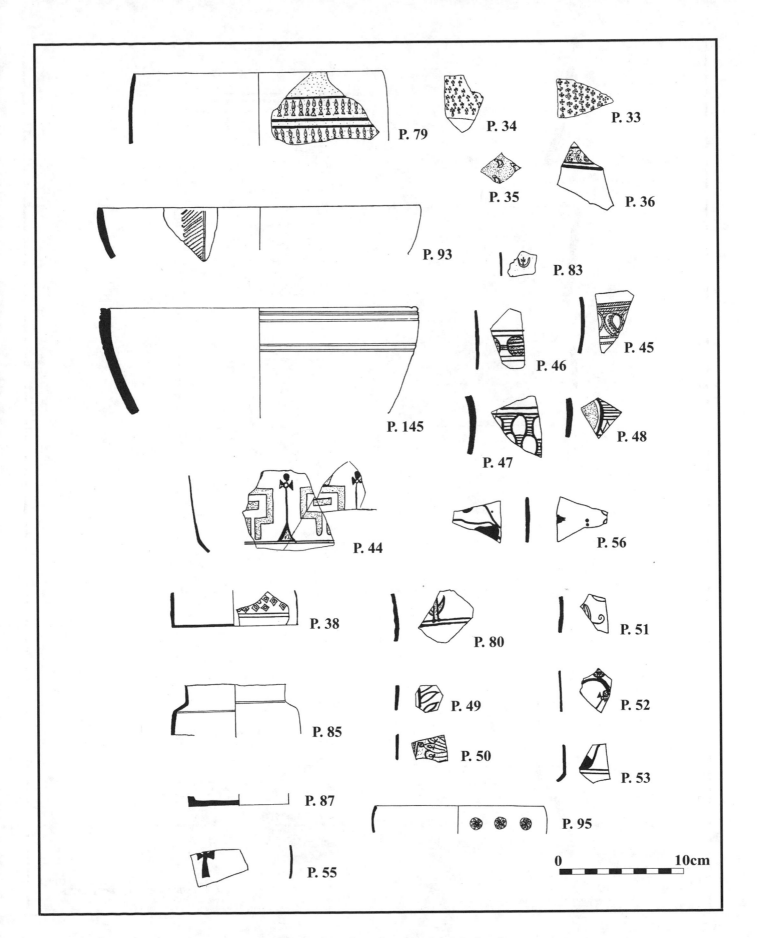

FIGURE 25. Fine ware bowls and sherds

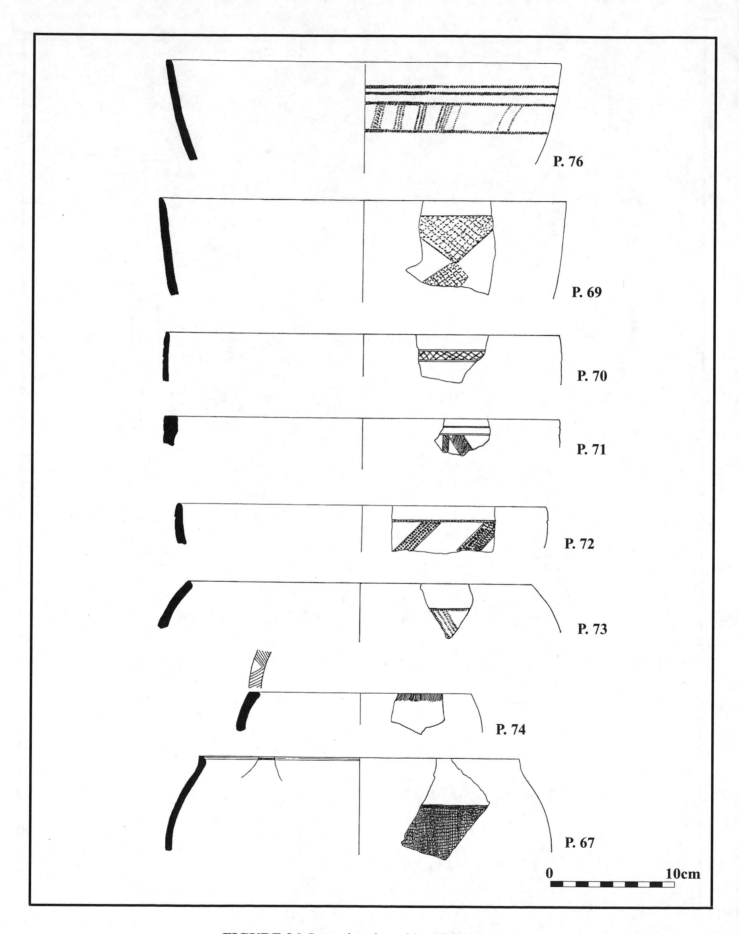

FIGURE 26. Large bowls and jars (black wares)

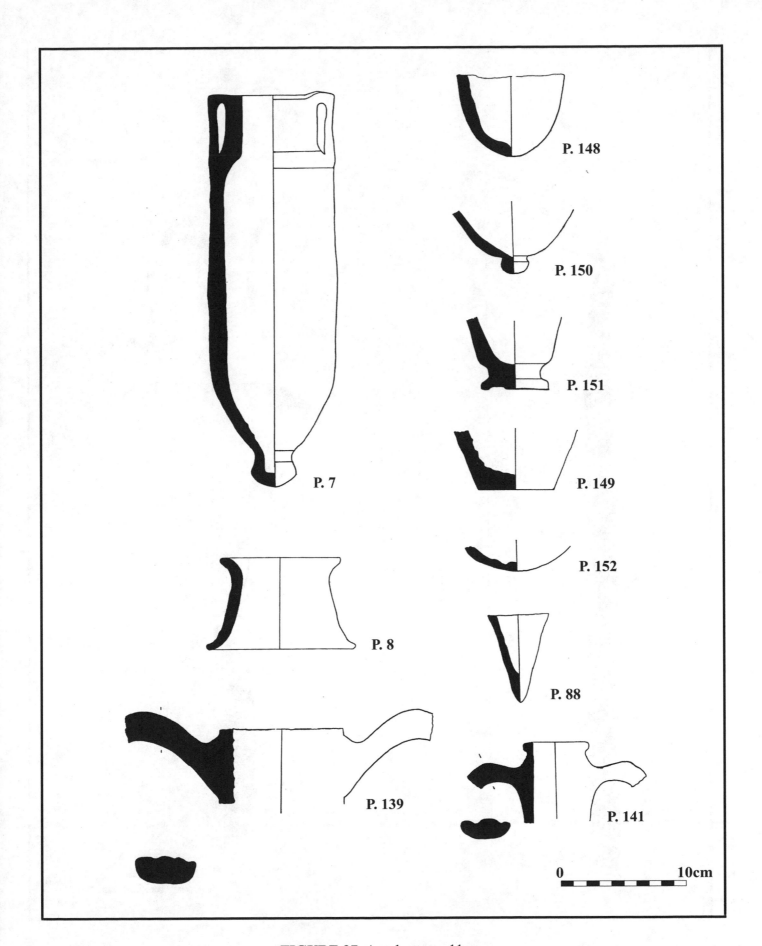

P. 148

P. 150

P. 151

P. 149

P. 152

P. 7

P. 88

P. 8

P. 139

P. 141

0   10cm

FIGURE 27. Amphorae and bases

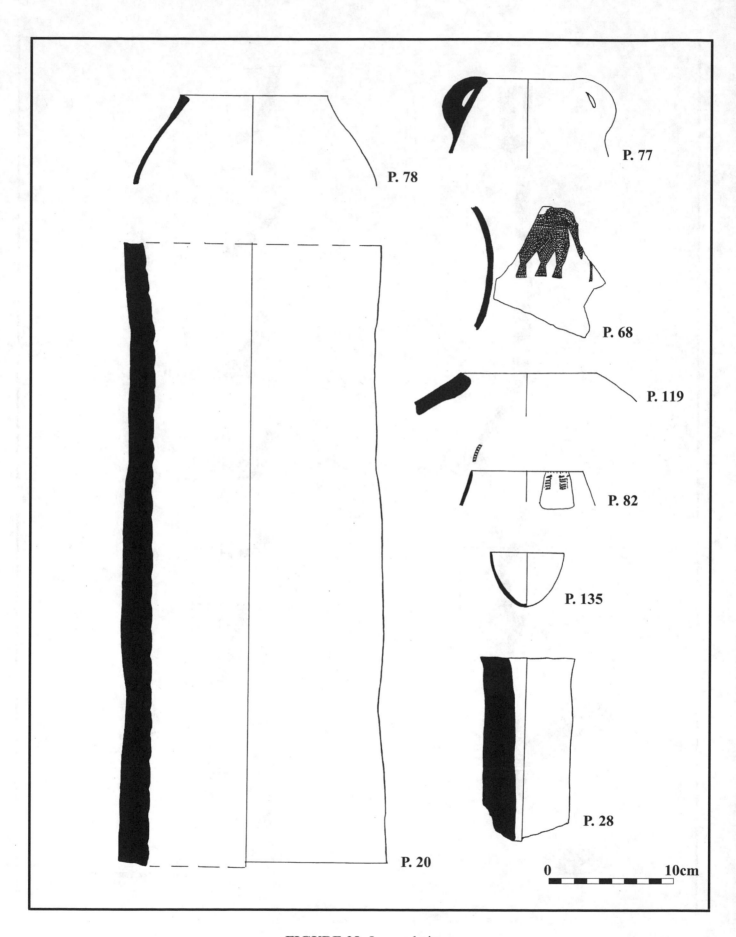

FIGURE 28. Jars and pipes

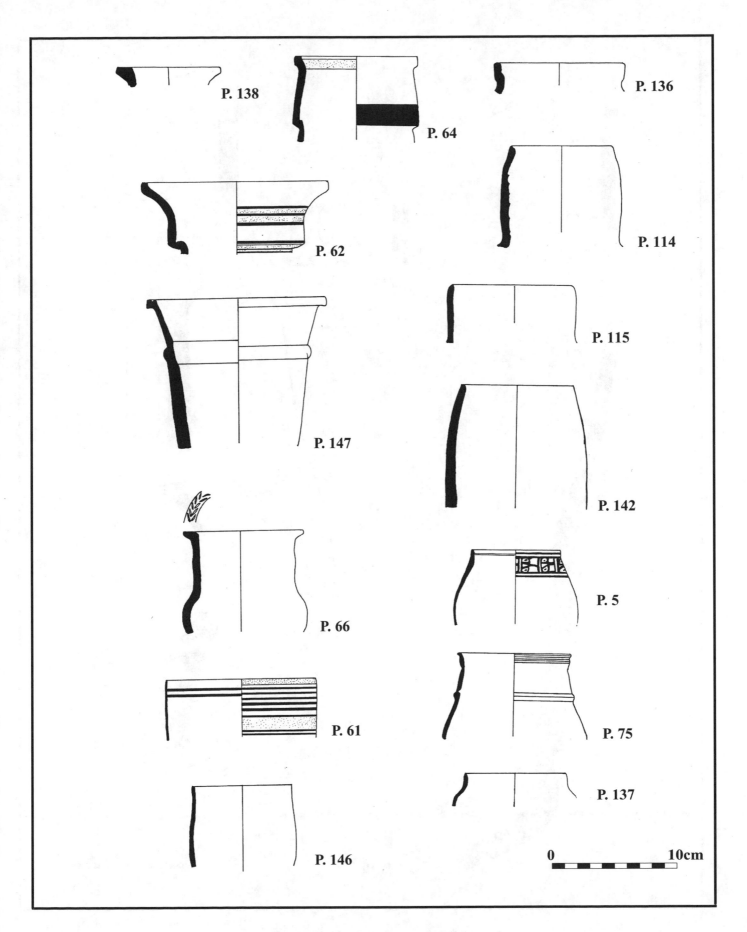

FIGURE 29. Bottles and beer jars

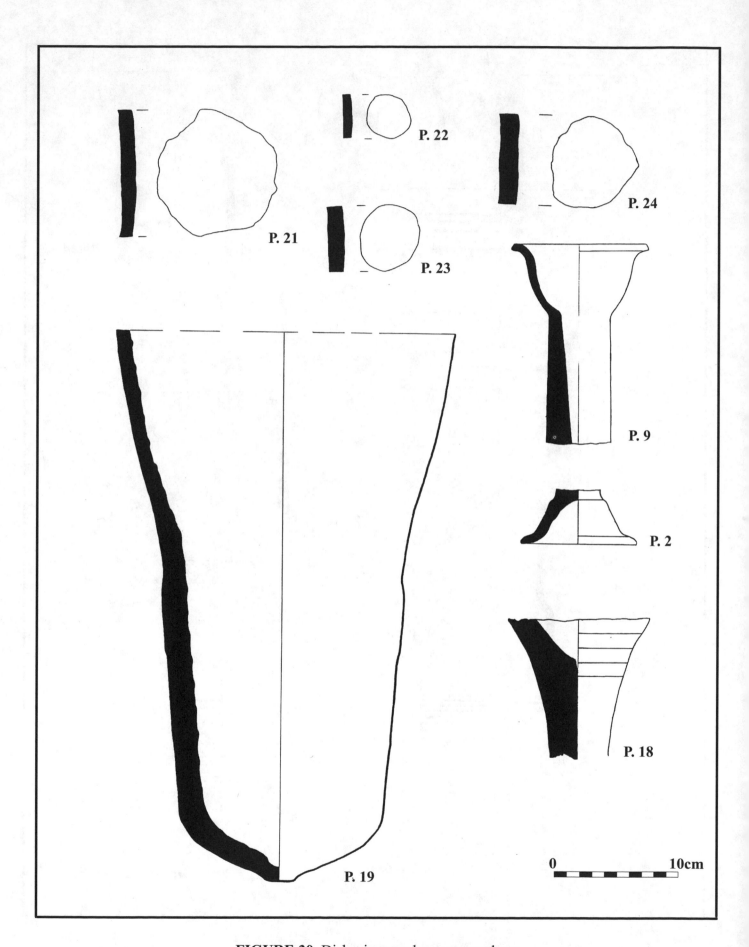

FIGURE 30. Disks, incense burners, amphora

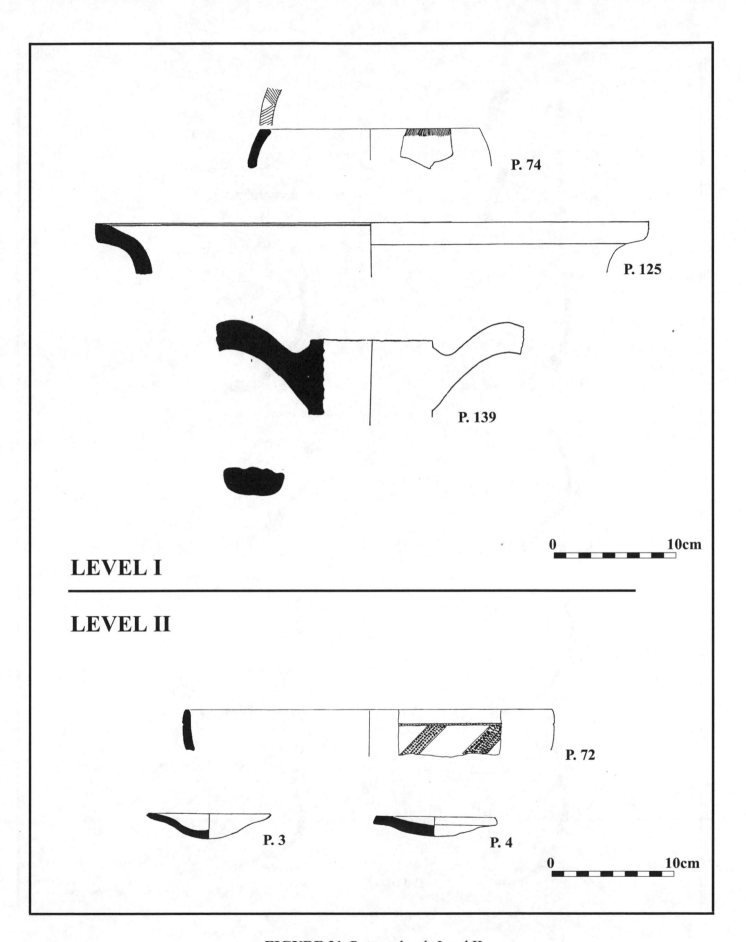

P. 74

P. 125

P. 139

0   10cm

LEVEL I

LEVEL II

P. 72

P. 3

P. 4

0   10cm

FIGURE 31. Pottery, levels I and II

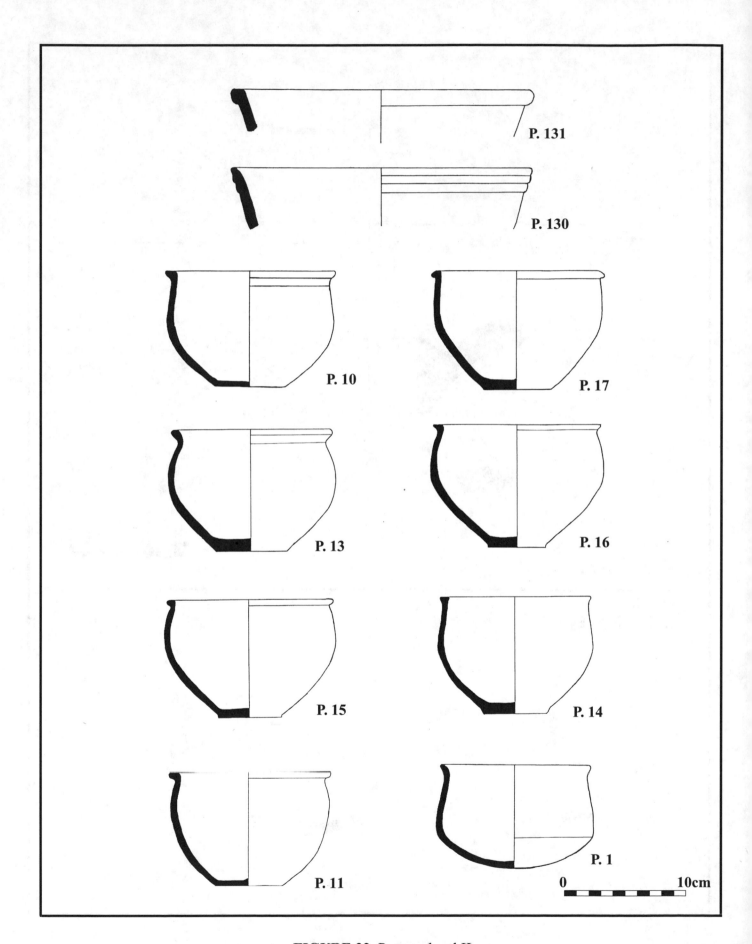

FIGURE 32. Pottery, level II

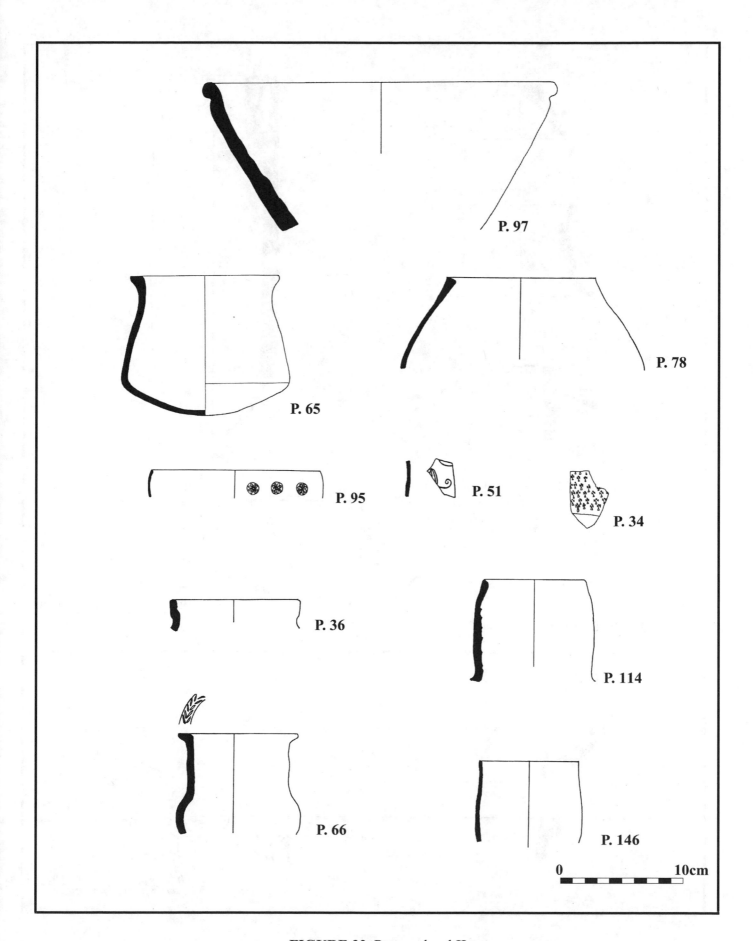

FIGURE 33. Pottery, level II

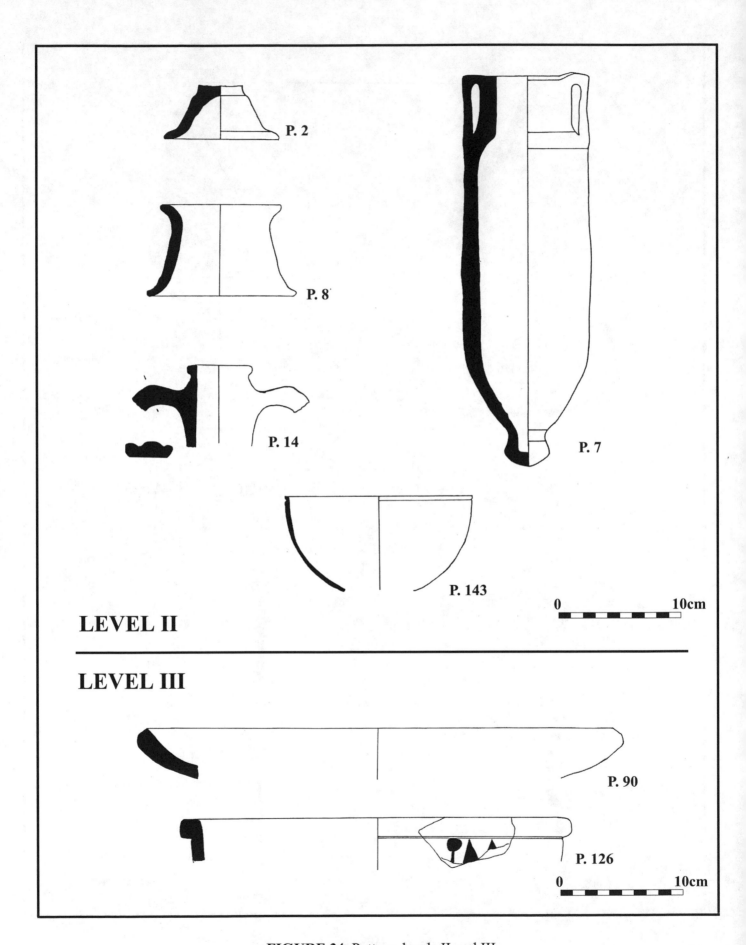

P. 2

P. 8

P. 14

P. 7

P. 143

0   10cm

LEVEL II

LEVEL III

P. 90

P. 126

0   10cm

FIGURE 34. Pottery, levels II and III

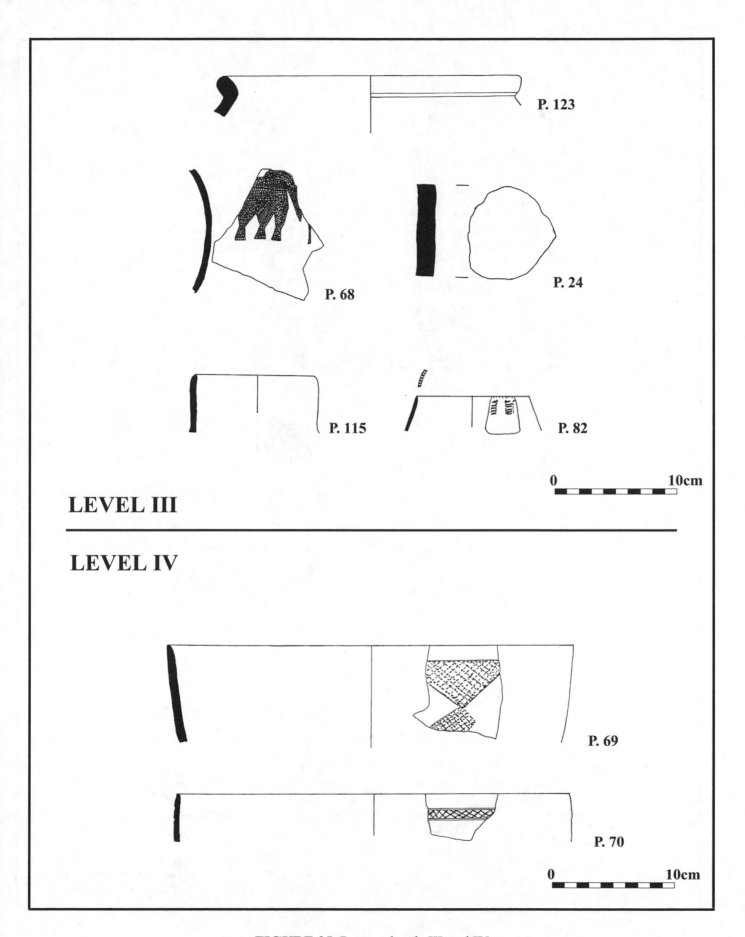

P. 123

P. 68

P. 24

P. 115

P. 82

0   10cm

LEVEL III

LEVEL IV

P. 69

P. 70

0   10cm

FIGURE 35. Pottery, levels III and IV

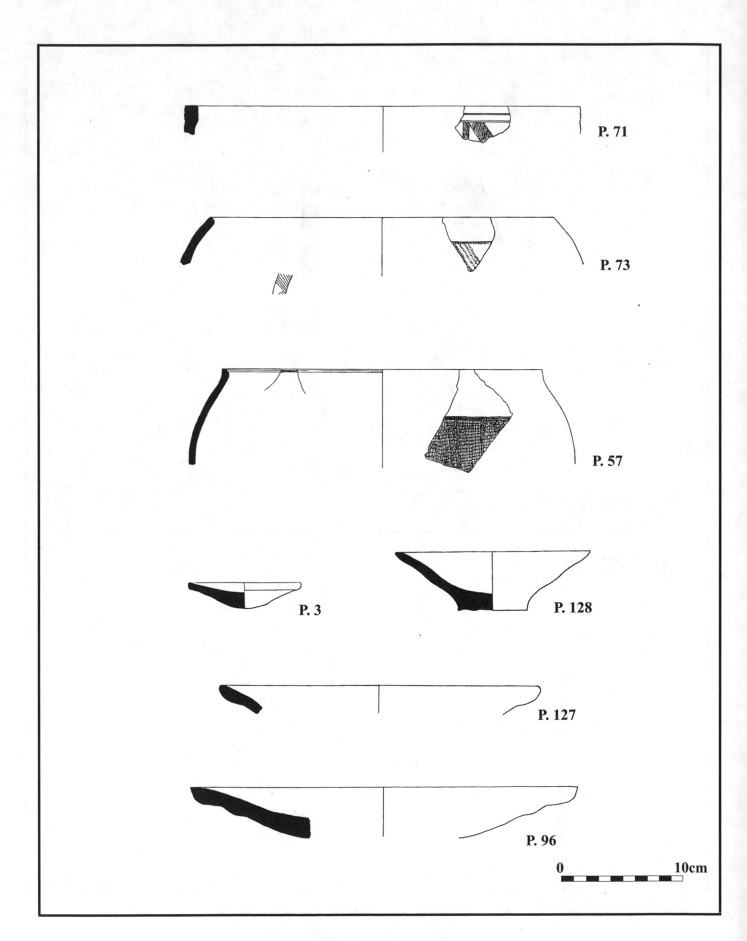

FIGURE 36. Pottery, level IV

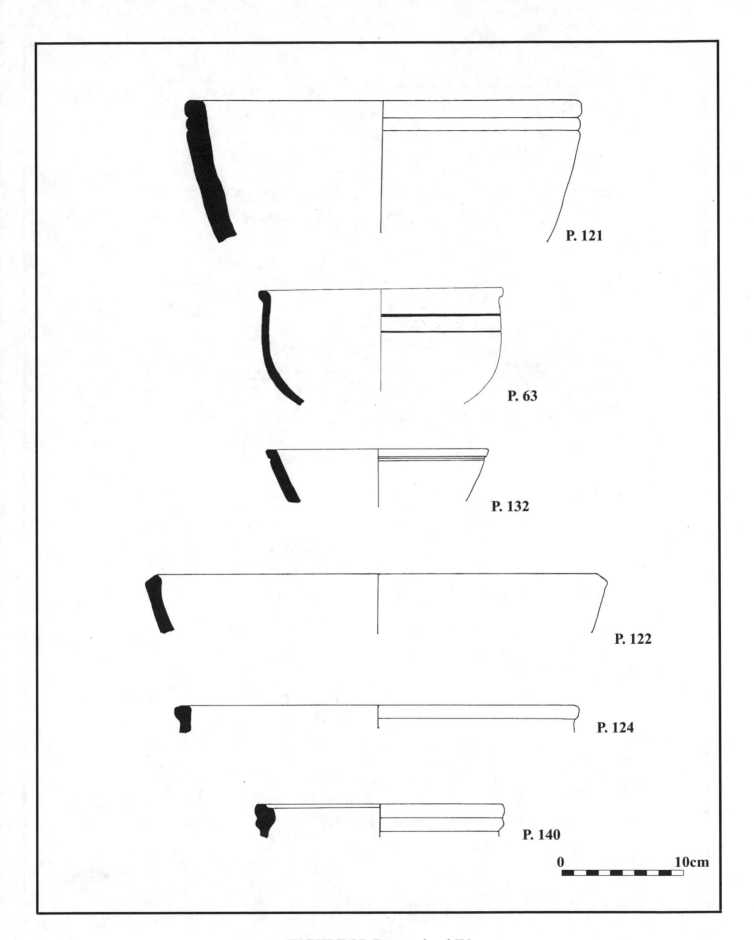

FIGURE 37. Pottery, level IV

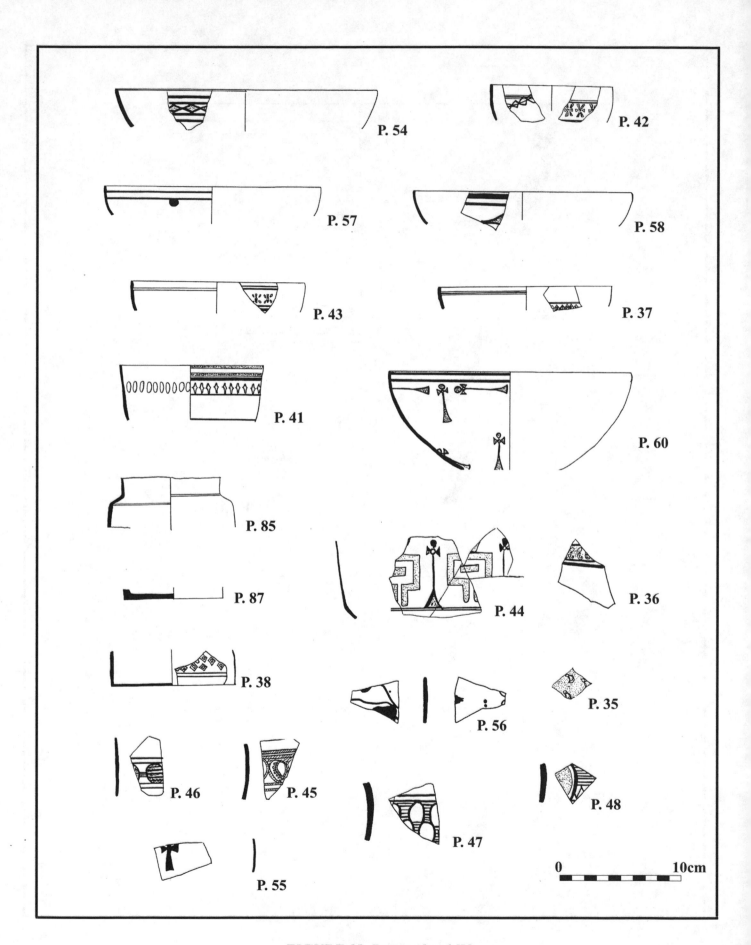

FIGURE 38. Pottery, level IV

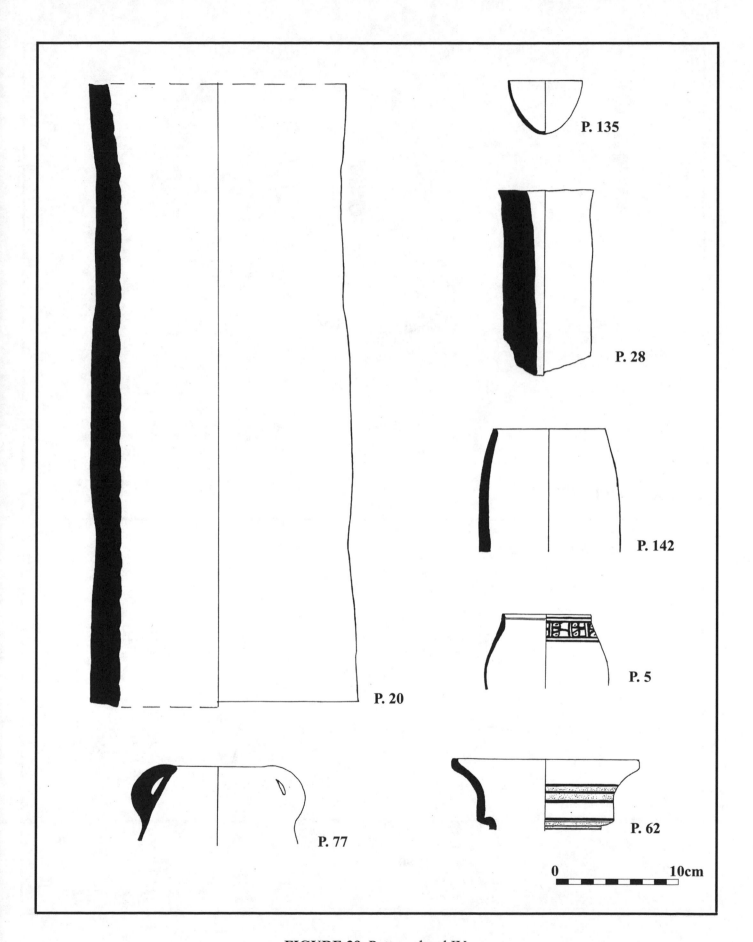

P. 135

P. 28

P. 142

P. 5

P. 20

P. 77

P. 62

0   10cm

FIGURE 39. Pottery, level IV

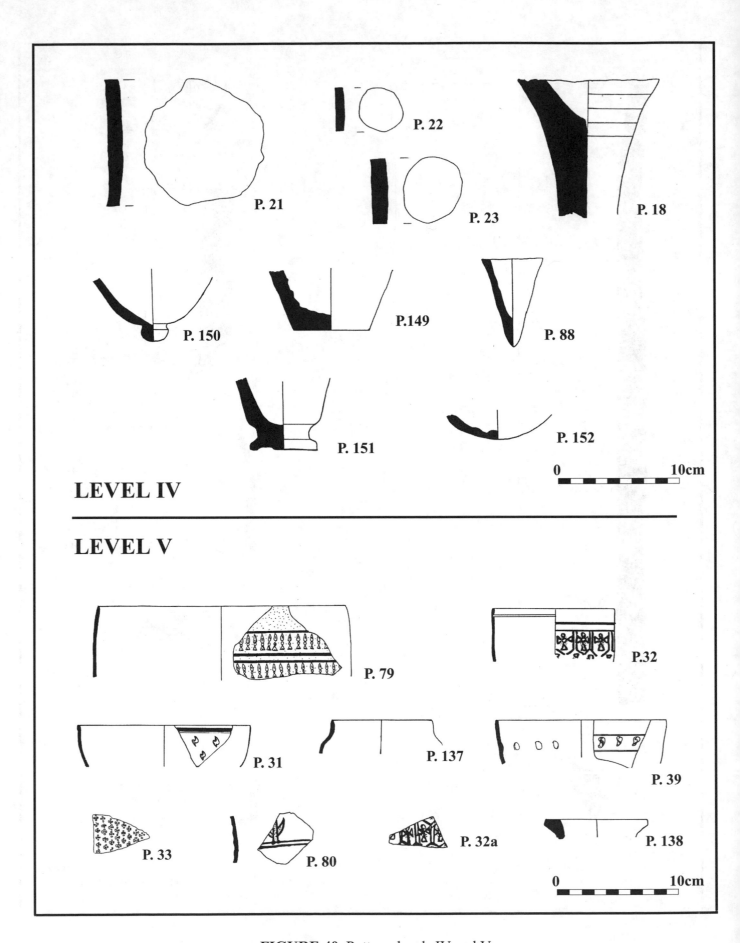

FIGURE 40. Pottery, levels IV and V

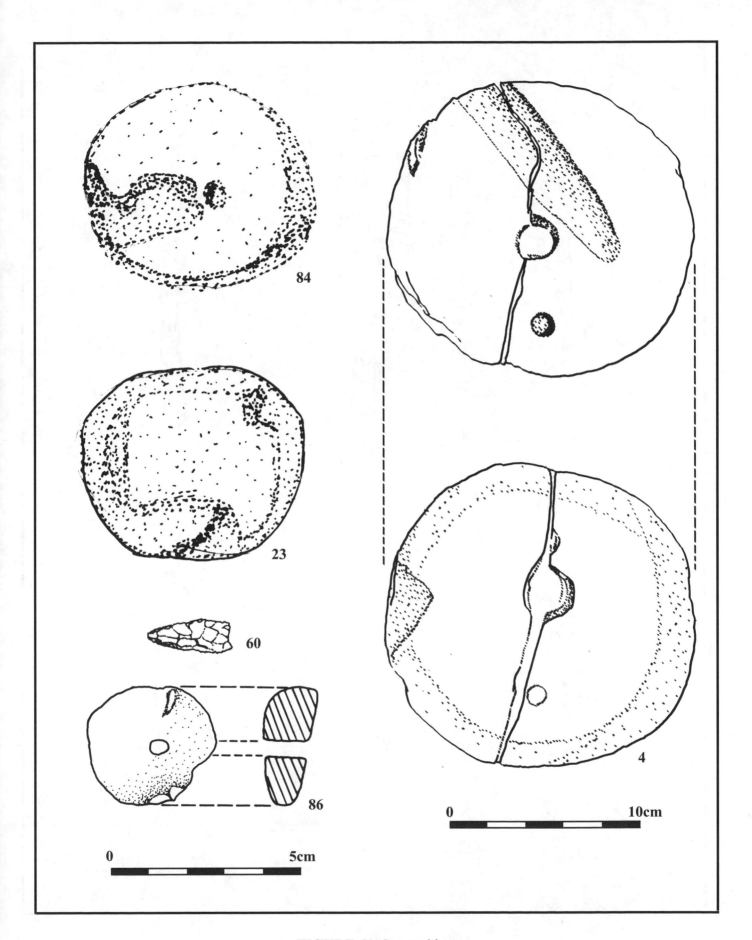

FIGURE 41. Stone objects

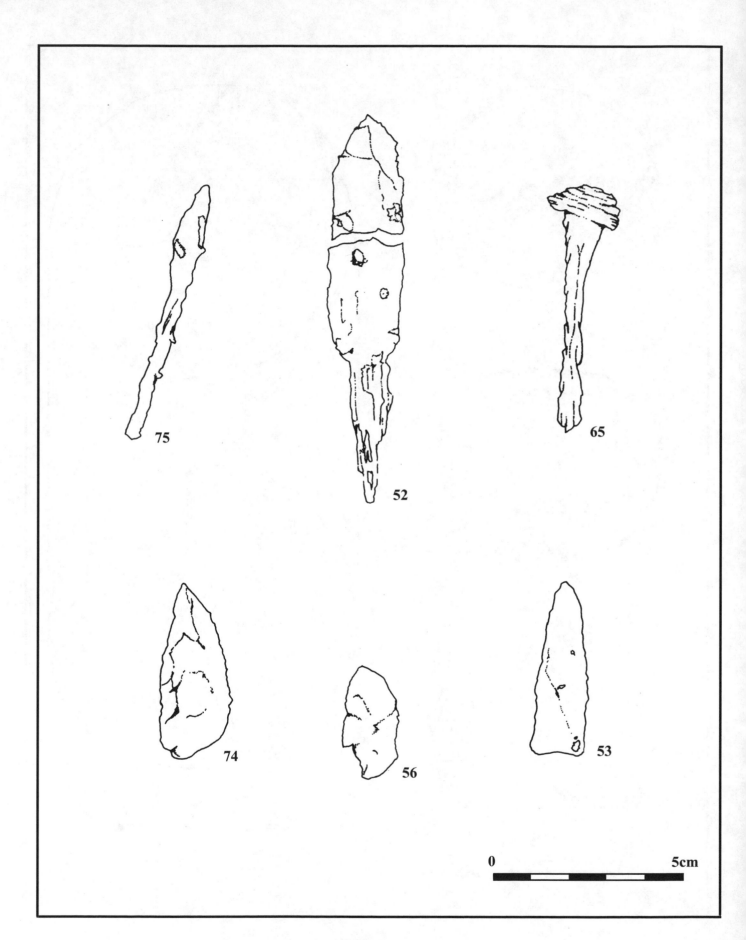

FIGURE 42. Iron objects

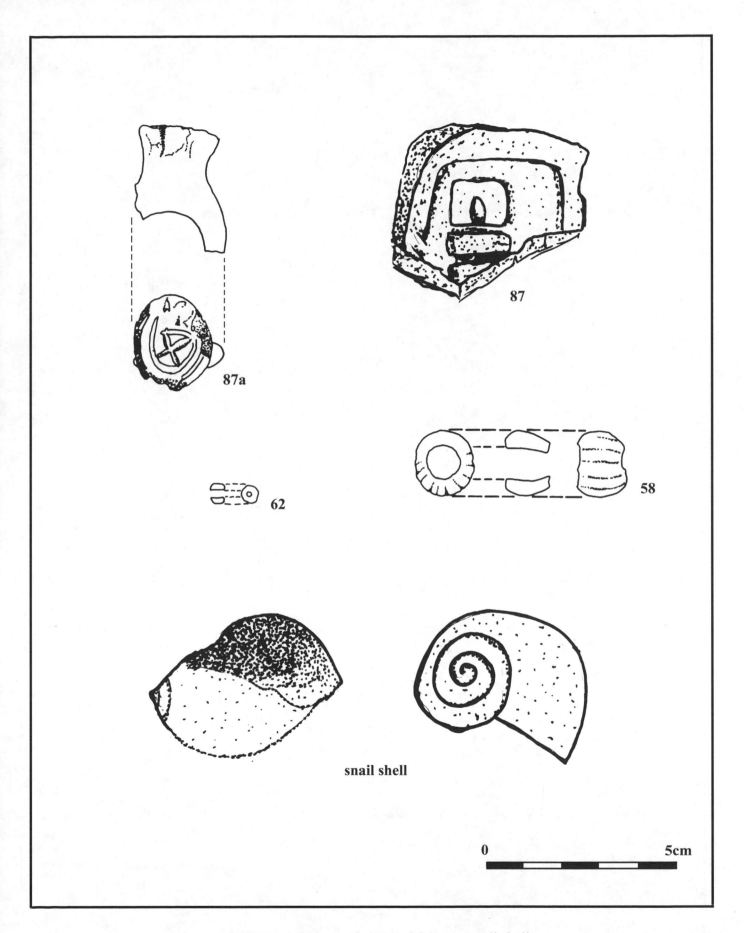

FIGURE 43. Objects of clay and faience; snail shell

a. Amun Temple entrance before excavation

b. Oblique aerial view of M 260 (photo B.-N. Chagny 2002)

PLATE I

a. Amun Temple, looking east, before cleaning

b. Amun Temple, looking east, after cleaning

PLATE II

a. Amun Temple, AT 5 before excavation

b. Amun Temple, entrance and north pylon after excavation

PLATE III

a. Amun Temple, AT 1, north face

b. AT 1, relief decoration

PLATE IV

a. AT 2, west face, relief decoration

b. AT 1, west face, relief decoration

PLATE V

a. AT 4, east face of the north pylon

b. AT 4, reconstruction of the north pylon

PLATE VI

a. Amun Temple, south gate, AT 39 (left) and AT 40 (right)

b. Amun Temple, south staircase AT 21, looking east

PLATE VII

a. Cultural deposit AT 35 within staircase AT 21

b. North staircase AT 20, looking east

PLATE VIII

a. Door blocking AT 47, looking west

b. Large bricks with finger lines, from AT 45

PLATE IX

a. Junction of walls AT 26 (left, with white plaster) and AT 29 (right)

b. Wall AT 26 and amphora emplacement AT 37

PLATE X

a. Trench A, looking north, M 279 in the foreground (photo P. L. Shinnie)

b. Trench A, looking north, stylobate in the foreground (photo P. L. Shinnie)

PLATE XI

a. M 271, relief block

b. M 271, north gate, sun disk and uraei

c. M 271, south gate, relief with feet

d. M 271, relief block

PLATE XII

a. M 271, relief block

b. M 271, relief block

c. AT 35, pot P. 9

d. M 271, *tashit*

PLATE XIII

a. Room M 266a, looking north, blocked door to M 269 in the back

b. AT 16, east face, Meroitic inscription

PLATE XIV

a. AT 17, south face, graffiti

b. AT 16, south face, graffiti

PLATE XV

a. Mound 712 before excavation, looking south

b. M 712[9], looking east

PLATE XVI

a. M 712[10], looking north

b. M 712[10], finds

c. M 712[4], looking east

PLATE XVII

a. M 712, late occupation, contexts 21, 22, 11 in the foreground, room "B" in the back

b. M 712, central part of the excavated area, looking north

PLATE XVIII

a. M 712, east part of unit 1, looking south

b. M 712, room "E", and walls 13 (left), 81 (back), 90 and 91 (front), looking southwest

PLATE XIX

a. M 712, wall 46, looking south

b. M 712, walls 51 (left) and 31 (right), looking west

PLATE XX

a. M 712, excavated area, looking northwest

b. M 712, walls 63, 43, 42 and stones 56

PLATE XXI

a. M 712, walls 43 and 63, looking south

b. M 712, unit 2, looking east, goat skeleton in the foreground

PLATE XXII

a. M 294, inside stone gate, looking north

b. Cartouche of Anlamani found near M 295

PLATE XXIII

a. Ledge-rimmed bowls

b. Fine ware pottery, painted exteriors

c. Fine ware pottery, painted interiors

d. P.44 with painted decoration

e. *Terra sigillata*

f. Red wares P.143 (left) and P.144 (right)

PLATE XXIV

a. Sherds with rouletted decoration
P.69, P.73, P.72 (top), P.76,
P.76a (middle), P.75a (bottom)

b. Sherds with incised decoration
P.70, P.71, P.74 (top),
unnumbered (bottom)

c. Supposed early pottery, P.71,
P.74 (top), unnumbered (bottom)

d. Bottles P.62, P.64 (top),
P.63 (bottom)

e. Amphora P.7, potstand P.8

f. Oyster shells from M 712[39], [45];
snail shell from M 712[74]

PLATE XXV

a. Loom weight no. 4

b. Millstone no. 72, grinding palette no. 73

c. Stone pounders nos. 45, 15, 3,
23 (top), 14, 18, 17, 16 (middle),
6 (bottom)

d. Palettes or grinding stones nos. 42, 20,
10, 47 (top), 8, 9, 19, 41 (bottom)

e. Arrowheads nos. 53, 52, 56, 74, 75

f. Faience plaque no. 87

PLATE XXVI